quiet leader, LOUD RESULTS

How Quiet Leaders Drive Outcomes
that Speak for Themselves

ANKIT MAHADEVIA

A POST HILL PRESS BOOK
ISBN: 978-1-63758-289-3
ISBN (eBook): 978-1-63758-290-9

Cover design by Cody Corcoran

Post Hill Press
New York • Nashville
posthillpress.com

Published in the United States of America
1 2 3 4 5 6 7 8 9 10

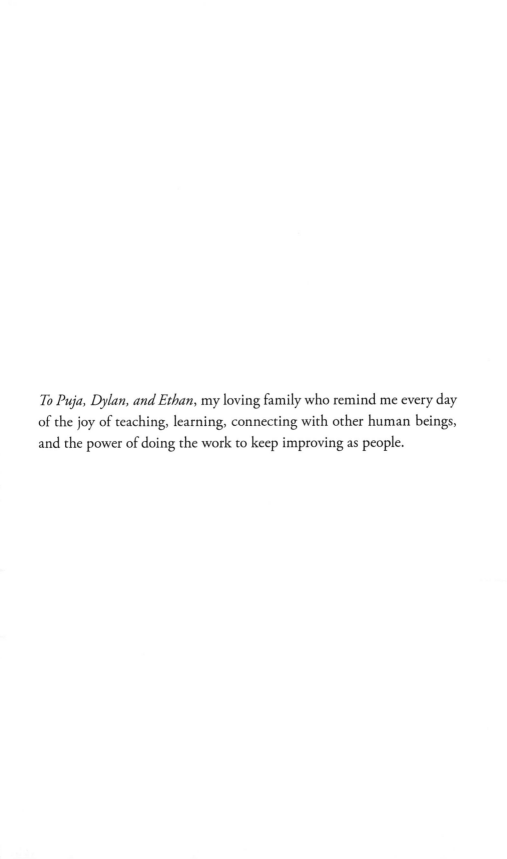

To Puja, Dylan, and Ethan, my loving family who remind me every day of the joy of teaching, learning, connecting with other human beings, and the power of doing the work to keep improving as people.

Contents

Acknowledgments

I'd like to thank the many quiet leaders across a range of industries who shared their stories as a part of this book. Some of my contributors prefer to be "closet introverts" and share their stories anonymously. I will gratefully acknowledge the other contributors directly: Chip Clark, Rahul Chaturvedi, Matt Johnson, Polly Murphy, Lionel Leventhal, Tim Clackson, Senator Will Brownsberger, Tim Herbert, Vicki Sato, Aoife Brennan, John Mendlein, Bill Cervino, Willy Shih, Jeb Keiper, Mike Gilman, David Sable, Kevin Cuthbert, Michael Useem, and Daniel Janel. Your willingness to share your ideas will help the next generation of leaders shape organizations they care about in the most authentic and effective ways possible.

I am also grateful to my partners "in the trenches" at the companies we have built together. Our experiences working together have been instrumental in shaping the philosophy behind this book. First, my colleagues on our company leadership teams: Cristina Larkin, Tom Parr, Tim Keutzer, David Melnick, David Grayzel, Paul Miller, Art Krieg, Dean Falb, Marty Jefson, Sath Shukla, Jamie Brady, and Tamara Joseph. Second, I am grateful for my advisors and Board members, who have shaped the principles behind this book through their mentorship and by giving me the space to learn through doing: Milind Deshpande, Patrick Vink, Frank Thomas, Peter Barrett, Jean Francois Formela, Bruce Booth, Reza Halse, Scott Jackson, Krishna Yeshwant, Vineeta Agarwala, Casper Breum, John Pottage, Vikas Goyal, Marian Nakada, Matt Cohen, Ed

Mathers, Josh Resnick, and Cynthia Smith. Special thanks as well to Jeff Stone, who has helped me become a better leader and find a style that works for me and that I can share here. Finally, I am grateful to Luke Timmerman for his intellectual contributions to the book, for sharing his formidable talents as a writer in reviewing a draft of the manuscript, and for raising my game as a writer in our collaborations together.

Introduction: An Introvert's Journey to Leadership

Entrepreneurs are natural outsiders. They look at the world and think about ways it could be made better. They come up with novel strategies and bring enthusiasm and drive that attracts others to the mission. They're undeterred even when the skeptics say it can't be done.

That's the positive side of being an outsider. But being an outsider can be both a blessing and a challenge to overcome for an entrepreneur.

In some ways, I've been preparing for this challenge my whole life. Growing up and as a young professional, I was always labelled as quiet and hard to read. I've always felt out of sorts at parties, often more comfortable inside my head and with ideas than with the loud, unpredictable nature of large gatherings of humans. I've long been the quiet guy in these settings—with friends, at school, or in a professional setting. Being the quiet person in the room has usually meant ceding the mantle of leader to others. It was easier, felt more natural, and left less room for doubt and embarrassment.

For years, in college and even into my early professional life, I was ashamed of how I allowed my introversion to prevent me from stepping up as a leader. I felt that my quiet nature was costing me the career milestones I wanted to achieve. I became determined to change myself. Early on in this journey to become a leader, I threw everything into practicing how to behave less like myself and more like the extraverted leaders I saw climbing the ladder. I tried to compensate for my quiet nature—forcing myself to "get out there," reviewing book after book on how to grab some of the momentum of social and professional interactions that came naturally to my extraverted colleagues. I even joined an improv comedy troupe to get in the habit of more spontaneous and animated interaction.

I thought it worked for a while. But as a worker bee, it always took a lot of extra energy to present myself as a "leader." I was more comfortable supporting others on the team. I was able to get things done by playing to my strengths in crunching numbers, reviewing scientific articles, and being an effective second fiddle in group discussion with experts. I thought I was hiding my more limited capacity for personal interaction and quiet nature well.

But at some point, I realized that I was hitting a ceiling. As an aspiring young associate at a venture capital firm, when I was given my long-awaited shot to actually join a company board, I was drained by the effort it took to be the louder, forceful, extraverted person that I thought I needed to be. Nobody was fooled. Rather than get into the flow of strategic conversations that didn't follow a predictable path, I was waiting for the right moment and for the perfect thing to say. Of course, the moment would pass, and I missed out on the crucial moments in meetings. I wasn't able to make a compelling case for my own strategic ideas. At best, I looked mute. At worst, I looked lost.

The dissonance between how I was leading and where I wanted to be in my career started to affect my confidence and my career outlook. I had specific expectations—that I wasn't meeting—about the impact I could have for my organization if I was "on track." My mentors, to their credit, were aware of my limitations and tried to help with well-meaning feedback. "Get out there more," they'd say. "Don't play it so close to the vest." They meant well, and I tried to follow their advice. I responded by doubling down on projecting as the type of leaders I read about who were charismatic, loud, self-assured. As my wife will tell you, I wasn't born the most emotionally attuned person, but even I could sense that persona wasn't authentic for me, and it wasn't going to work.

My wake-up call came one day. I was leading a group of experienced scientists several decades older than me on a project to test a treatment for muscular dystrophy. The science was new, untested, and uncertain. We had to triangulate the needs of a demanding inventing scientist and a rigid large pharmaceutical company that was our collaborator in order to keep the project funding going. We needed at least $1 million to get the key experiments done. While our investor gave us some startup funds, we needed all collaborators to agree and finalize our relationship. Then, we ran into some fairly typical obstacles. An experiment didn't go as planned. A disagreement between collaborators over something small escalated into something big. The inventor went radio silent. The company didn't get off the ground.

In moments of tension and challenge, as I know now from experience, a leader finds a way to build the resilience of the team, communicate, meet people at their level, settle them down, and solve the issues at hand. In this case, everyone, from the inventor to the scientists to my mentors and investors, headed for the exits when the project ran into some typical challenges. This opportunity for me to lead ended in an avoidable failure.

People on the team gave me some blunt feedback. It was a gift, even if it hurt at the time. The lead scientist didn't think I was doing a good job. She wasn't shy in sharing this perception with my mentors. Hearing this negative feedback secondhand was painful (and probably should have been handled differently by the scientist). In hindsight, this was exactly what I needed to get past this cycle of trying to outwork my quiet nature as a leader.

The short version: the depth of my communication and style did not engender the vision, passion, and trust needed to keep the team together through adversity. The team had a sense that I wasn't sharing all of the information, that maybe I was holding something back. Trying to be a different kind of person didn't help matters. It finally happened: trying to "get out there" and use a style that wasn't authentic became extremely detrimental to my effectiveness as a leader.

Getting the ball taken away stung badly. But it was a wake-up call I needed. I didn't want to give up my ambition to lead an organization that brings medicines to patients, but if I was going to achieve this goal, I knew I needed to come up with a new way to lead that was a better match for my personality. The way I was doing things wasn't working, and it wasn't going to work.

Somehow, despite my setback, I was given another shot to build more companies. I resolved to do something different. Since then, I've helped form nine biotechnology companies. These companies have delivered FDA-approved medicines for patients, advanced many more into human trials, executed on three initial public offerings, and inspired larger pharmaceutical firms to invest and collaborate with us. One of these nine companies grew to become Spero Therapeutics, which I lead today. The journey at Spero has been a thrilling ride, from the founding in 2014 with just a $400,000 investment to discovering our first medicines, to going public, to advancing our medicines in clinical trials.

It has also been a journey of tremendous growth for me and a complete transformation of my mindset. I went from seeing my personality as something to hide to one that gave me strength. I realized that there was no one way to be an effective leader. I learned to embrace my own authentic style and bring the best of who I am to my organizations.

This book is for fellow introverts and quiet folks to have an alternative to the lonely, exhausting, and ultimately ineffective strategy of trying to act like the (particularly American) extraverted ideal of a leader. I have been where you are, frustrated at not being as effective as I can be, and drained every night as I tried to copy the extraverted ideal of a leader. As I have continued my career in business and talked to many dozens of quiet leaders for this book, it turns out I'm not alone.

Chapter 1

The Quiet Leader's Struggle

Who do you picture when you think of a dynamic leader that inspires people to join them, invest with them, and follow them? Chances are it's someone who's outspoken, gregarious, energized by large and small group interactions—a classic extravert. These traits are also what we associate with those destined to rise up the ranks and become the leaders of tomorrow.

However, most of us (a recent survey suggests nearly 60 percent) are introverts—people who are not energized by social interaction and who need less stimulation from people around us.[1] There are also many extraverts who just aren't gregarious or outspoken by nature. People from either group with "quieter" personalities (we refer to them as "quiet leaders") might be labeled as aloof, intense, hard to read, or worse yet, not as competent as our extraverted peers.

[1] Melissa Summer, "Introverts and Leadership: World Introvert Day," The Myers-Brigg Company, 2020, https://www.themyersbriggs.com/en-US/Connect-with-us/Blog/2020/January/World-Introvert-Day-2020.

Charles' Story:

Charles loved many parts of his job as CEO of a drug discovery startup—studying the science, building a team, and executing a strategy. Yet he dreaded the annual pilgrimage to Miami for one of his investor's annual meetings. His fellow CEO colleagues looked forward to it every year—attendees included hedge fund managers, CEOs of large pharmaceutical companies, and high-potential executives looking to join the next great startup.

Theoretically, one could (and many CEOs did) network for days and even well into the nights over dinner, drinks, and after-hours parties. As an introvert, Charles felt drained each night after doing his best to match the energy of his colleagues. On top of being on empty, he felt he let his business down as other CEOs kept pushing forward, and he felt that his peers and the organizer of the meeting were judging him for not doing as much as he could. It also seemed as if he was the only one, that being an introvert wasn't compatible with the image of a successful leader. This feeling both of exhaustion and feeling not quite good enough was not a sustainable place for him to exist. He needed to find a way to make these required parts of cultivating followership for his business sustainable.

Charles is far from alone. Many quiet leaders who work hard, know their stuff, and bring value to the table are stymied by what their peers and superiors assume about their competence and ability to drive results. Company leaders often notice the people who speak up in meetings and pay less attention to the quieter people in the room. The perception of a quiet leader (or their fear of being perceived) as an aloof, intense, less competent professional can prevent many from reaching their leadership ambitions. These perceptions have real consequences as aspiring quiet leaders strive to move up the ladder in the leadership structure. In a 2006 survey, 65 percent of senior corporate executives viewed introversion as a barrier to leadership; other studies have showed the correlation between perceived effectiveness and extraversion, including one study looking at U.S. presidents.[2]

Further, the idea that a different, less extraverted style needs to be accepted and effective is critical in a society that's increasingly diverse—not just across neurotypes but also across gender and culture. Many organizations are making investments to try to build a leadership structure that reflects the diversity of the world around them. For this change to occur, companies will also need to rethink some longstanding perceptions about the personality traits of effective leaders.

Further, companies should recognize how these misperceptions about leadership dovetail with preconceived notions about women and minorities to add extra barriers to advancement. Quiet female leaders should not have to contend with the misconception of being soft or not decisive enough. Quiet leaders of other cultures should not have to contend with misconceptions about their command of the language or their assertiveness. In this way, diverse leaders who are quiet leaders are "double outsiders" by virtue of their background and how they interact with the world (we will explore the intersection of quiet leadership with being part of another group underrepresented in leadership in Chapter 9). Well-meaning advisors who focus on superficial fixes to help a double outsider "fit in"—a cultural outsider's accent or wardrobe—are missing

---

[2]   Adam Grant, Francesca Gino, and David Hofmann, "The Hidden Advantages of Quiet Bosses," *Harvard Business Review*, 2010, https://hbr.org/2010/12/the-hidden-advantages-of-quiet-bosses.

an opportunity to help these leaders be effective and still be their best, authentic selves. New frameworks of understanding effective leadership are needed today, as an increasingly diverse group of leaders (including many quiet leaders) will lead best if they can lead in their own authentic way rather than trying to copy an extraverted style.

A Better Way

So how can those of us with quieter personality characteristics rise to lead at the organizational level? Many of us feel forced to "fake it" when we lead in a world full of extraverts or forgo leadership opportunities entirely because we think, "That's not me." The pressure to fit into the ideal affects many of us—a recent UK survey suggested nine out of ten people reported feeling pressured to act in an extraverted way.[3]

The issue is further complicated by the limited nature of most "advice for introverts" books, workshops, and general messaging. Introverts tend to get the same (well-intentioned but unhelpful) advice, i.e., "Just practice networking, you'll get used to it!" "Stop overthinking it, just do what needs to be done," or "Get over it." In other words, again, *fake it*. That kind of advice demonstrates that many people—including some introverts themselves—profoundly misunderstand quiet leadership and expect introverted and other types of quiet leaders to conform to the extravert's world if they want to hold senior leadership and C-Level positions.

This is not a sustainable solution—not for quiet individuals and not for the organizations they serve. Introverts who assume leadership roles without an authentic style risk burning out and hitting a ceiling on their effectiveness. Many more who cannot harness their unique strengths may never be tapped to lead at all. Organizations that allow this to

---

[3]   Melissa Summer, "Introverts and Leadership: World Introvert Day."

happen are not getting the most out of their work force, and individuals who suffer this fate could be getting more fulfillment and velocity from their careers.

The consequences of trying to fake it for too long can be insidious; they can lead you (they did for me) to feel that something's missing from your career, and you never feel quite "good enough." They can also be larger, even for those that manage to succeed spectacularly at pretending to be an extravert. The concept of "introvert burnout" or "introvert hangover" is real, and the draining nature of pushing yourself to have social interaction after social interaction can affect those quiet leaders that identify on the introverted side of the scale.[4] Sometimes, this burnout can be quite visible. Neil Rudenstine, president of Harvard University from 1991 to 2001, was brave enough to go public with his severe case of burnout.[5] He made some important changes in his life to combat this, including reducing his grueling fundraising schedule.

The good news is that these barriers do not have to hold quiet leaders back. This is a book by a quiet leader for current and aspiring quiet leaders, building on the experiences of experienced quiet leaders who have road-tested different ways to be effective without being the loudest person in the room. It is for all of us who do not identify as extraverts (or who don't possess the "louder" traits that many associate with leaders) and explores the why and the how of becoming a dynamic leader on our terms. Through this book, I will explore real world examples from effective introverted leaders. I hope to demonstrate how to exercise leadership at an organizational level in a style authentic and adaptable

---

[4]   Shawna Courter, "Yes, There is Such a Thing as an 'Introvert' Hangover," IntrovertDear.com, August 11, 2016, https://introvertdear.com/news/yes-there-is-such-a-thing-as-an-introvert-hangover/.

[5]   Karen Arenson, "A Harvard Leave Highlights Pressures of University Life," *The New York Times,* 1994, https://www.nytimes.com/1994/12/04/us/a-harvard-leave-highlights-pressures-of-university-life.html.

to your unique strengths. The strategies in the coming chapters, and the real-world examples that reinforce them, offer an alternative to "faking it" in a world used to a more extraverted leadership style.

Along with it being possible to be both quiet and an effective leader, it is critically important for quiet leaders to take on greater leadership. Indeed, achieving leadership goals is good for the quiet leader for sure, but it's also desperately needed in our world. An increasingly multi-cultural, technology- and science-intensive, fast-moving society needs a diversity of thinking and personality types among its leaders. We're better off as a society if quiet leaders can take their rightful leadership roles and bring the balance of thinking styles needed to make sound, forward-looking, and audacious decisions. The data suggest that quiet leaders are highly effective, if only they choose and are chosen to lead. The CEO Genome Project looked over ten years at the effectiveness of over seventeen thousand C-suite executives across multiple quantitative measures. They found that the quiet leaders in the survey actually met their board's expectations *better* than did their extraverted counter-parts.[6] The next Microsoft, Google, or Berkshire Hathaway—each an introvert-driven organization—is less likely to develop when there are barriers to leadership for quiet leaders. As further evidence of the power of quiet leaders, some high-profile organizations have thrived as extra-verts have passed the torch to quieter leaders (think Jobs to Cook at Apple, Ballmer to Nadella at Microsoft, and Kalanick to Khosrowshahi at Uber).

I've grown tremendously in my comfort, confidence, and authen-ticity as a leader. I've marveled at how far I've come when, both for this book and in my day-to-day work, I surprise people who have precon-ceived notions of what being a quiet leader means, with my presenta-tions, interpersonal interactions, and transparency. This book aims to

---

[6] Elena L Botelho, et al., "What Sets Successful CEOs Apart," *Harvard Business Review*, 2017, https://hbr.org/2017/05/what-sets-successful-ceos-apart.

be a practical primer to help you grow in your comfort and authenticity as a leader. While the science that explains *why* quiet leaders are unique support the strategies in this book, I encourage aspiring leaders to focus on the actions from real-life examples that illustrate *how* quiet leaders can present authentically and effectively.

This book will review:

- How quiet leaders carry themselves in different settings of leadership
- What unique strengths and key limitations they often bring to leadership
- The key activities of leadership and how introversion affects the way in which quiet leaders practice these activities
- How introverts can lead most effectively through each of these activities
- Where to go from here

Chapter 2

Are You a Quiet Leader? Unpacking What Quiet Leadership Means for You

The Economist reports that over 25 percent of leaders identify as introverts.[7] However, being a quiet leader can be lonely as our (particularly American) culture is both dominated by and aspires to extraversion. Quiet leaders don't tend to advertise their nature because this personality trait is neither celebrated nor rewarded. Often, leaders have spent years honing their ability to appear extraverted. Knowing how to imitate extraverted leadership doesn't mean that you are leading from your best and most authentic self. Indeed, knowing the answer to a few key questions is critical in identifying how best to show up for your team and organization:

- Are you a quiet leader?
- If so, what are your unique strengths and weaknesses that come from quiet leadership?

---

[7] Kate Rodriguez, "Leaders, Consider Your Introverts," Economist Education (*The Economist*), https://execed.economist.com/career-advice/career-hacks/leaders-consider-your-introverts.

- Are those who you lead, or those who lead you, quiet leaders? How do you know, and what does this mean for you?

With these answers in mind, you can begin the work of building your authentic way of working with others that fits for your personality type.

Who are Quiet Leaders?

Quiet leaders may have similar characteristics externally. However, the source of their quiet leadership can come from different personality characteristics. We will focus on a few personality types under the umbrella of quiet leader:

- Introverted leaders
- Quiet ambiverts/extraverts
- Other personality traits that tend to quiet leadership

A history lesson: The literature on introversion and extraversion is relatively new, and evolving. One of the original theories on personality types comes from the twentieth-century Swiss psychiatrist Carl Jung. Jung's simplistic view of personality was one of binary archetypes. He defined extraversion as "an outward turning of libido" and introversion as "an inward turning of libido." In other words, the distinction is driven by where energy is directed: internally or toward the world around us.[8] Over the coming decades, new researchers and even Jung himself began to accept that introversion and extraversion are part of a continuum, and that a third category—ambivert—is a place many people identify. This

---

[8] Elaine Houston, "Introvert vs Extrovert: A Look at the Spectrum and Psychology, PositivePsychology.com, January 26, 2022, https://positivepsychology.com/introversion-extroversion-spectrum/.

melding of the distinction between introverts and extraverts continues today, and some researchers have posited that no specific personality types exist—only a continuum.[9]

While introversion is a continuum, there is a biological basis for the personality differences between introverts and extraverts. With the advance of diagnostic technology, researchers have documented differences in the brain chemistry and activity of people with different personality types. In other words, your personality type can be correlated with which parts of your brain are more active than others, including how you react to pleasant and unpleasant images. This supports the idea that some parts of personality are innate (though can be modulated over time).[10, 11] Further, scientific studies have shown that extraverts need more stimulation to achieve levels of neurotransmitters associated with well-being, and they seek this through more stimulating experiences such as social interaction.[12] That feeling of being overstimulated as a quiet leader after a few hours in a loud cocktail party also has a basis in how you are wired.

Our focus is on leaders who tend more toward the introvert side of the spectrum, whether these leaders are true introverts, ambiverts, or even considered somewhat extraverted. There are related traits of shyness and sensitivity that are worth examining as well. Shy and sensitive individuals manifest as quiet, but they do so for different reasons. Shy people can be extraverts or introverts; the key difference between shy individuals and introverts is the comfort with which they engage socially

[9]   Ibid.

[10]   Lisa Trei, "Happy Faces Trigger Different Brain Reactions in Extroverts and Introverts," *Stanford Report*, 2002, https://news.stanford.edu/news/2002/july10/sciencegab-710.html.

[11]   Xu Lei, Tianliang Yang, Taoyu Wu, "Functional Neuroimaging of Extraversion-Introversion," *Neuroscience Bulletin* 31, no. 6 (2015): 663–75 https://www.ncbi.nlm.nih.gov/pmc/articles/PMC5563732/.

[12]   Marti Olsen Laney, *The Introvert Advantage: How Quiet People Can Thrive in an Extrovert World* (New York, NY: Workman Publishing, 2002).

when they choose to do so. Introverts are comfortable in social situations but require replenishment after such engagements. Shy individuals may ultimately find interactions either energizing or draining once they engage, but anxiety limits their ability to engage.[13] Another important distinction is permanence: introversion is a trait that is intrinsic. It can be modulated, but it is not a phase that individuals cycle in and out of. Shyness is less permanent; in fact, a famous study noted that over 80 percent of people surveyed noted being shy at one time in their lives.[14] Sensitivity is a trait that is also sometimes associated with introversion; these individuals exhibit heightened reactivity to stimuli, whether visual, auditory, or emotional. By nature, sensitive individuals will gravitate toward lower intensity settings as introverts often do, but for different reasons. Further, 30 percent of sensitive individuals in a recent study also identify as extraverts.[15]

Regardless, whether introverted, shy, or sensitive, quiet leaders with any of these traits will embrace different leadership styles than the extraverted leader ideal. Many of the same strategies that work for introverts can be applied to the other types of quiet leadership. The quiet leaders we profile span all three types of quiet leadership. Now for the practical part—how do these theories of personality and sources of quiet leadership apply to you and the people around you?

---

[13]   Success as an introvert. Joan Pastor PhD. Wiley 2014.

[14]   Ibid.

[15]   Daniela McVicker, "9 Things I Wish People Knew About Me as a Highly Sensitive Extrovert," Literally Darling, https://literallydarling.com/blog/2019/07/22/highly-sensitive-extrovert/; Jacquelyn Strickland, "Introversion, Extroversion and Sensitive Person," The Highly Sensitive Person, April 24, 2018, https://hsperson.com/introversion-extroversion-and-the-highly-sensitive-person/.

Making it Practical—How to Identify Yourself and Others as a Quiet Leader

What follows is a practical "reading people" definition that put together the views of many of the quiet leaders in this book, including my own. There are instruments, like the Myers-Briggs evaluation and others, that can—in a systematic and validated manner—help identify where you stand on the "E" versus "I." Solely relying on these is somewhat impractical; obviously, you can't give a Myers-Briggs to everyone you meet. Further, in assessing yourself, the diagnostics can be helpful (I'm an INTJ for what it's worth), but overreliance on them can be misleading. Assessment results change over time as you change and provide a binary label for a personality trait that's a continuum. Further, no quantitative instrument is perfect; Myers-Briggs's characterizations of personality have been shown to sometimes change between concurrent administrations of that diagnostic to the same individual.[16]

Some caveats before we dive in

The art of identifying quiet leaders is imperfect. It takes personality clues that emerge over time to really have a good read on a person. It pays to approach the art of identifying personality types with some humility. Even as a purported expert on quiet leadership, I have more than once been shocked in having conversations for this book to learn that a supposed extravert was actually a closeted introvert.

A few "grains of salt" to take with your initial read of others and of yourself:

---

16 Gregory J. Boyle, "Myers-Briggs Type Indicator (MBTI): Some Psychometric Limitations," *Australian Psychologist* 30 (1995): pp. 71–74, https://doi.org/10.1111/j.1742-9544.1995.tb01750.x.

- **The continuum**—As discussed there is not a black or white introvert versus extravert, and most people in the leadership setting are selected for having at least some balance through the hiring, credentialing process.
- **Situation dependency**—Depending on the audience, the stakes, and what else is going on in a person's life, a person may present at one point or another on the scale of behaviors that make for an introvert or extravert.
- **Stress**—Stress pushes all of us to default to how we actually are as our reserves to hide our perceived flaws melt away. The median stress level in your leadership situation will impact how and when people show up; for example, in a trauma bay versus a corporate board room. This median stress level may or may not be the same as the "getting to know you" process you used to make your assumptions.
- **Incentives**—Many introverts have learned over time to "fake it," particularly in the critical getting to know you phase of beginning to work with a team. As we've discussed, introversion is not necessarily a celebrated trait in the culture of business leadership.

What matters

What matters, then, is how a person shows up in the sphere that you most frequently interact with them and at the operational intensity level most common to your leadership setting. It may be true that your introvert colleague (or you) come to life among friends and family, but if in a professional setting you present as a quiet leader, this is what matters. So, what questions should you be asking of yourself or those around you to identify a quiet leader?

Tom—the "obvious introvert."

Viewing my co-founder Tom's accomplishments on paper, one might reasonably assume that he is an extravert. A philosophy major in college and microbiologist by training, Tom had been leading hundreds of people for most of his career. He led an entire research division, started a number of companies, and built large research teams (including ours at Spero). He has been instrumental with his colleagues in presenting his companies' science and convincing investors and partners to finance each of these enterprises. At Spero, he was part of a senior team that helped us raise over $150 million and was a core part of selling the story as we took the company public in 2017. However, within thirty seconds of first meeting Tom, you would know he's as quiet a leader as there is in any industry. Tom makes no pretense of being an outgoing leader. He notes that he is of Scandinavian descent and that you can tell an extraverted Scandinavian by "whose shoes he looks at when they're talking." He is understated to the extreme. Tom was infamous among our infectious disease community for "sloping" or leaving cocktail parties or even long meetings when his tank was empty after social interaction. After a few months of working with him, I learned when possible, to avoid having our one-on-one meetings after 4 p.m., as typically Tom needed to recharge by then after a day of interactions. Still, through a combination of experience, humor, deep concern for others, and passion for our mission, people follow Tom, and have gotten to know and trust him.

We will revisit what makes Tom effective as a quiet leader in later chapters. His classic (and obvious to most) traits provide a jumping off point to get a read on yourself, and those around you. A few questions to consider:

- Do they get energized by human interaction in the professional setting more often than they are drained by them?
  o At the end of a long day of business meetings, are they ready for drinks or ready for dinner alone?
- After a busy day, are they more or less engaged with you? At the end of a long interview process, are they still chatting up members of the team, or are they saying their goodbyes and heading out the door?
- Do they need unstructured interaction to work things out or come to you when thoughts are more formed?
- In a debate or over a controversial issue, are they opining loudly and often, or infrequently, thoughtfully, and less noticeably?
- Where do they stand at being able to "read the room" and shift their views based on nonverbal cues? Does their energy mirror your energy closely or does it stay steady regardless of your affect?
- Do they prefer to communicate topics in a larger group or 1:1?
  o In an unstructured way or in a structured way?

If you or your colleague is taking "Option B" more often than not, they are likely a quiet leader. A great time to observe where someone is on the continuum in the setting where you collaborate with them is in between meetings or discussions—this is likely a better read of where they stand versus when they are focused on the task at hand (and can summon the energy to channel some aspects of extraversion). For those wanting to go deeper, there are a variety of quizzes (such as Adam Grant's quiz[17]) that can provide an imperfect but useful triangulation of personality types.

It's important to note that visible personality traits are a quick diagnostic of how a person presents; they also signal a different way of processing the world. This mental construct is usually less evident when you are trying to get a read on someone, but over time is even more important as to how you collaborate with a quiet leader. We will dive into these different ways of processing the world later in the book. They will be important as we explore how to make sense of the world around us as a quiet leader (Chapter 3) and run our teams that have a mix of extraverts and quiet leaders (Chapter 5).

So now you've identified yourself or a leader you collaborate with as a quiet leader. Why does this matter? How does this define how you show up as a leader, and how you can get the most out of your leadership?

What Are Strengths of Quiet Leaders?

The misconceptions and limitations aside, quiet leaders have many assets that support strong leadership. They are worth amplifying, as too often introversion and related traits are seen as something to hide. In fact, in seeking contributors to this book, several did not want to advertise their introversion because of their fear that it would cast aspersions on their ability to lead. We will visit how to leverage these strengths for specific practices of leadership in later chapters. Let's examine a few:

---

[17]   Adam Grant, PhD, "Quiz: Are You an Extrovert, Introvert or Ambivert?" Ideas.Ted.Com, March 29, 2018, https://ideas.ted.com/quiz-are-you-an-extrovert-introvert-or-ambivert/.

- **Listening skills**—In speaking to extraverts and introverts alike, this is a core driver of good leadership that comes naturally to quiet leaders. Social science research has also explored this phenomenon; a recent study in Sweden used quantitative measures of listening as they followed a cohort of introverted and extraverted managers and found that the quiet leaders exerted more listening effort and engagement.[18] These findings make intuitive sense as well. Quiet leaders, by virtue of being more contemplative and speaking less, naturally create space for others to speak, creating room to make people feel heard, hear new ideas, and let creativity flourish. We will discuss in later chapters how to use listening skills and your natural inclination to leave space for others to your advantage as you run your team, connect with key constituents, and communicate your message.

- **Capacity for reflection**—Introverts spend more time reflecting on their thoughts before sharing them and more time reflecting internally as they restore after social interaction. This is correlated to findings in neuroscience: studies have shown that introverts demonstrate higher neuronal activity in areas associated with learning, planning, and information processing than do extraverts.[19] This reflection allows for deep thought and refinement of decisions and discussions outside of the heat of the moment. As we'll discuss, this can enhance a team's creativity and ability to think strategically. We will examine this further as

---

[18] Anna Emanuelsson and Sandra Lindqvist, "Leadership of Introverts: An Exploratory Study of How Introvert Managers Lead in Sweden," Blekinge Institute of Technology (Faculty of Engineering, April 21, 2014), http://bth. diva-portal.org/smash/record.jsf?pid=diva2%3A831842&dswid=3760.

[19] Joseph Bennington-Castro, "The Science of What Makes an Introvert and an Extrovert," Gizmodo, September 10, 2013, https://gizmodo.com/the-science-behind-extroversion-and-introversion-1282059791.

we explore how quiet leaders can learn about the world around them and then strategize accordingly (Chapter 4).

- **Internal locus of idea creation**—This capacity for listening and reflection means that a quiet leader is more influenced by internal consideration and reflection, and less so by external stimuli and interaction. Many psychological studies have identified the internal locus of control that quiet leaders often possess, and the correlation of this inward-looking trait with positive attributes, such as a steadfastness in the face of external variability, and the capacity for deep thought and creativity.[20]

  o *Perception of steadfastness*—One such trait that flows from an internal locus of control is a steadfastness despite external noise. Quiet leaders, often whether they like it or not, tend to present as lower key regardless of what is going on around them. In emergencies and other periods of stress and uncertainty, teams look to leaders for reassurance and for cues on how it is appropriate to react. The lower modulation of a quiet leader's emotions can be hugely beneficial as they can radiate calmness, confidence, and defuse stressful situations. Many quiet leaders who contributed to this book note that even when they feel out of control, they are amazed by how little people around them can tell. This great strength, however, can also be a disadvantage when teams look to you to acknowledge and validate their emotions in difficult situations; we will tackle this more in Chapter 5.

  o *Creative thought*—Multiple studies have explored the correlation between introversion and creativity. These studies

---

[20] Rose Needle, "Innovative and Introverted: How Introverts Function in the Creative Workplace," University of South Carolina (Honors College) 2019, https://scholarcommons.sc.edu/cgi/viewcontent.cgi?article=1292&context=senior_theses.

find a correlation between individuals with introverted traits and creative traits. Quiet leaders tend to look inward for guidance and generation of thought, and this deep introspection allows for original thought and creativity. Too much inward-looking thought, of course, and some of these great ideas may never be heard or executed upon, so we will explore how to find the balance in the coming chapters.[21]

Quiet Leaders: Limitations

There are limitations to leadership that quiet leaders must overcome, as we saw in Mike's example in the previous chapter. Some of these are real limitations, and many of these are amplified in preconceived caricatures of whether introverts can lead effectively. We focus on some of the ones that the quiet leaders in this book have faced, and the coming chapters will address how to account for these.

- **Limits on social interaction**: Leaders are expected to be force multipliers, making organizations around them and people around them better. The ability to have repeated, consistent social interactions can certainly facilitate this. For example, the work of selling one's mission and vision either in repeated one-on-one meetings or in large group settings can be exhausting for a quiet leader. An extraverted CEO raising money for her startup may be invigorated after a day of meeting new investors; a quiet leader may be drained. Even if this is not the case, the perception that quiet leaders are less effective in social

---

[21] G.J. Feist, "A Meta-Analysis of Personality in Scientific and Artistic Creativity," *Personality and Social Psychology Review 2* no. 4 (1998): pp. 290–309. https://doi.org/10.1207/s15327957pspr0204_5.

interaction influences who boards and managers put in charge of people (see selection bias below).

A corollary to social interaction limitations is input bias. Extraverts that form ideas and generate energy by interacting with people have an opportunity to refine their ideas in a way that reading and/or research may not. Extraverts more naturally find that unique "nugget" of insight leaders sometimes gain through conversation. We will cover how to best learn about the world in which you lead through a variety of inputs, including high quality interactions with experts, in later chapters.

- **Volume bias:** The principle of the "squeaky wheel gets the grease" applies here. Traditionally, an extraverted phenotype is able to get the most attention from superiors, customers, collaborators, and their reports just by controlling the social action. Quiet leaders can sometimes not be heard or their words disregarded. Indeed, social science confirms how quiet individuals' reticence to speak over others can impact collaboration—in studies of college classrooms and mandatory group projects, introverts performed less well and expressed more discomfort in social interaction. They saw benefits when allowed to work individually and express their views through writing instead of group interaction.[22] We will tackle how to win hearts and minds, and inspire action even without being the loudest person in the room.

- **Speed bias:** Quiet leaders, more likely to fully form a thought before delivering it and more prone to listen before they react, can sometimes form an opinion more slowly than an extravert. For leadership teams not attuned to different personality types, the extraverts may have shaped an important decision and the

---

[22] Maria Zafonte, "A Phenomenological Investigation of Introverted College Students and Collaborative learning," ProQuest Information & Learning, 2018.

team may have moved on before quiet leaders have had their say (more on how to manage this later in the book).

- **Fit bias**: Especially in particular industries and parts of the world, the ideal of a successful, effective business culture is one that trends extraverted. For quiet leaders entering these industries, they must fight harder to fit in (this was true in my own experience). At best, they are burning the candle at both ends to fit in, and at worst, they just don't make it in these cultures. Further, in an extraverted-led business culture, extraverts tend to prefer extraverts and perceive them to have higher potential as transformational leaders. Social science research supports the fit bias—transformational leadership studies suggested that extraverted traits were the primary predictor of *perceived* (but not actual!) leadership effectiveness.[23] We will spend Chapter 8 examining how to work best with our extraverted colleagues.

- **Selection bias**: The culmination of these potential differences is that quiet leaders may be less likely to be put in charge in the first place. A recent survey of four thousand executives showed that the more senior the title, the more likely that this cohort of leaders exhibited extraverted tendencies.[24] Worse yet is the internal monologue many quiet leaders face that drives them to opt out of leadership positions. An introvert who compares visible gusto for the mission to that of extraverted peers competing for dollars, talent, and customers creates a self-fulfilling prophecy. The fear, doubt, and uncertainty that an introverted approach is "enough" versus the extraverted leadership ideal makes it even harder to be effective.

---

[23] Timothy A. Judge, Joyce Bono, Remus Ilies, and Megan Gerhardt, "Personality and Leadership: A Qualitative and Quantitative Review," *Journal of Applied Psychology* 87, no. 4 (2002): pp. 765, DOI: 10.1037//0021-9010.87.4.765.

[24] Adam Grant, et. al, "The Hidden Advantages of Quiet Bosses."

So, What's Next?

We have reviewed some of the archetypes of quiet leaders—the intro-verts, the shy, and the sensitive leaders. Now, for aspiring leaders and those of us currently leading people and organizations, what to do about both unique qualities quiet leaders have and the strengths and weak-nesses they present?

What not to do

Nearly every introvert has been instructed to just try and "fake" extra-version; however, the "fake it until you make it" approach simply isn't sustainable. Introverts who push themselves to be someone they're not come off as being inauthentic (a quality no one wants in a leader) or eventually burn out from the mental energy required to maintain an extraverted façade. This energy which could be put to much better use for their organizations.

Kelly (name changed)—the closet introvert.

Kelly has been a leader in the competitive field of executive recruiting in technology. In a rapidly growing industry, every company is looking for the same talented, experienced candi-dates, and a talented recruiter can make all the difference to stand out. During my first interaction with Kelly, I was sold by the energetic way that she grabbed my attention even over the phone. She sustained this energy throughout our interactions, and former clients I spoke with mentioned it was one of her hallmarks. It was easy for me to infer that the candidates we'd hire her to pursue would be equally enticed to learn more about us (and we found this to be true). Further, it would stand to reason that in a profession that is all about interpersonal interaction, she would be an extravert. When I called her for potential referrals in her network for the book, she bowled me over by noting that she was an extreme introvert. Thinking about this further, I reflected upon her ability to listen very thoughtfully, the analytical way that she approached her assignments, and her preparation (all practices we'll dive into later in the book).

The downside of this is how each day leaves her exhausted—she needs a long time to recharge after a long day of interacting with candidates. While she is incredibly effective in her role, her limitations as an introvert have caused her to consider whether she'd be fulfilled in a more senior role that requires more overt self-promotion and affords less opportunity to control when and how she has to be "out there" interacting with others. Further, understandably, she declined to have her real name in the book given the misconceptions that many have about introverts in the recruiting profession. That said, she was certainly keen to have her thoughts contribute to dispelling this notion.

Kelly's story suggests that being a "closet introvert" is working for her for now—and if her ambition is to be in her current role, this is sustainable. However, if not, a quiet leader trying to fake it will ultimately hit a ceiling and either be asked to or decide to opt out of making a broader impact on an organization. Even if you have been able to become a good leader by pushing outside of your personality set, the sustainability of being someone that you're not is limited and is less effective as the scale, complexity, and intensity of a role grows.

So, Why Lead at All?

You may be at a crossroads where many quiet leaders find themselves—leading in the way that contemporary culture expects you to can be exhausting. Even worse, society tells us that quiet leaders aren't as desirable as extraverted ones. Why not let others do it and find another role within the organization? *It is because quiet leaders can be extremely effective leaders, but they just need to lead differently.*

Indeed, the fundamental premise of this book is that both *quiet leaders and extraverts can be equally effective leaders*, and in some very important circumstances, *quiet leaders can be even more effective*. Both early leadership research and our current biases about who can be effective play into preconceived (and inaccurate) notions of leadership as the primary domain of extraverts. Lord and colleagues did a meta-analysis (or systematic, methods-based review) of twenty-four studies on leadership effectiveness, finding that studies that purported a link between a leader's personality and organizational performance actually were linking those characteristics more to leadership emergence, or whether people *subjectively* think a leader should be leading rather than how the leaders actually did.[25] Other, more recent studies, such as by Adam Grant and colleagues, have found that on objective measures of performance like revenue, quiet leaders can actually perform better in important circumstances, such as when they have proactive, motivated employees.[26]

---

[25] Robert Lord, Christy de Vader, George Alliger, "A Meta-Analysis of the Relation Between Personality Traits and Leadership Perceptions: An Application of Validity Generalization Procedures," *American Psychological Association* 71, no. 3 (1986): pp. 402–410, https://psycnet.apa.org/record/1986-29983-001.

[26] Adam Grant, Francesca Gino, David Hofmann, "Reversing the Extraverted Leadership Advantage: The Role of Employee Proactivity," *The Academy of Management Journal* 54, no. 3 (2011): pp. 528–550 https://www.researchgate.net/publication/276054647_Reversing_the _Extraverted_Leadership_Advantage_The_Role_of_Employee_Proactivity.

So, what should a current or aspiring quiet leader do? We encourage you to take the next step in growing your leadership skills. In a world that's chaotic, where those you lead demand autonomy, respect, and agency, quiet leaders can be uniquely equipped for the challenges of leadership. We just can't practice leadership the way that our business culture thinks we should: we need to organize how we think about leadership differently, and then practice the art of leadership differently. The coming chapters begin this journey.

Chapter 3

A Roadmap for Quiet Leaders— Goals for Leadership and a Toolkit for Moving Forward

You've established yourself as a quiet leader, and you want to lead in a world that is made for extraverts. So where do you go from here? Like everything else that's complicated, breaking leadership down into components is a good place to start. Focusing on the components of leadership creates framework around your tendencies, the unique strengths you bring to each component, and some of the limitations to overcome as you bring your authentic style to the table.

Our leadership checklist breaks down the practice of leading an organization into four key components. These components are required regardless of whether you are leading a group of thousands or are an army of one. We will then show how the quiet leader can practice these most effectively. In building the checklist, we have chosen a pragmatic definition from my own experience and that of other quiet leaders. Further, we have chosen a broad definition—many, more specifically defined leadership activities (such as fundraising or managing risk) can be divided up among the categories we've chosen to define below.

The Quiet Leader's Checklist:

Whether you are leading as an army of one, or your organization has thousands of members, every leader spends some part of their day on a few key activities. Practicing these disciplines well is a hallmark of effective leaders:

- **Setting a Direction**—Understanding what's going on inside and outside of your organization, and using that understanding to set your strategic vision
- **Executing**—Turning this vision into stellar results that move your organization toward its goal
- **Connecting**—Winning hearts and minds to the cause on a one-on-one basis to support your mission
- **Building a following**—Winning converts to the cause inside and outside your organization on a larger scale

Setting a Direction

There are two parts to setting a direction within an organization:

- Understanding the world around you and within your organization
- Using that understanding to set strategy.

Information is everywhere, and understanding as a leader means getting access to all of the important information and separating the important data from the unimportant. Once you have a picture of the world around you, you can then create a vision and set plans accordingly.

There are many advantages to how quiet leaders approach setting a direction. Their ability to carefully listen and tendency to go deep in analysis can mean they can get more information out of a given conversation or set of data. Again, quiet leaders' neurophysiology correlates with this tendency, especially for introverts, who process signals (whether from people, books, or other areas) at a higher intensity than their extraverted counterparts.[27] Once a quiet leader has understanding, their unique strengths can help set strategy. Particularly for introverted quiet leaders, the ability to retreat, think, and put multiple pieces together in creative ways can yield better plans.

> *The quiet leader's dilemma:* I'm generally better than most about squeezing every drop of insight and inference from sources that don't require social interaction—news articles, scientific journals, social media discourse, what I hear as I walk around a conference (but not engaging in conversation!). Further, I have often been able to squeeze maximal insight from the discussions I do have by using my strengths as a quiet leader, such as intentional listening, introspection, and analysis. Also, I have done this out of necessity, as I found a way to adapt to my tendency to prefer less interpersonal interaction. This all said, I have always marveled at the way that extraverts can seemingly effortlessly add to their own dataset through targeted and untargeted conversations. More in my perception than in reality, I worry that these discussions give extraverts some sort of edge I'm not getting.

---

[27] Liz Fosslien and Mollie West, "6 Illustrations That Show What It's like in an Introvert's Head," *Quiet Revolution*, https://www.quietrev.com/6-illustrations-that-show-what-its-like-in-an-introverts-head/.

You may be wondering how quiet leaders can gain this understanding, from customers, employees, and others, when it is not written down? We will show how they can build this deep understanding of the world without having to use the brute force method of repeated social interaction, or by avoiding truly insightful conversations altogether.

We will cover how quiet leaders can build a deep understanding of the world around them without having to use brute force method of repeated social interaction, or avoiding truly insightful conversations altogether.

> *The quiet leader's dilemma:* Michael was in charge of a technical group developing products within a multi-national digital imaging corporation. Every year, he'd have to give a forward-looking view on the division's strategy in light of the company's objectives. After deep analysis with his team of trends, conversations with his customers, and work from consultants, he found that he was able to very efficiently arrive at what *should* be done to achieve his development objectives for the year. A quiet leader by nature, he feared that the hard part for him would be getting his team excited to put this plan in motion. Quiet leaders will not be ones to get people behind a plan with a charismatic "win one for the Gipper" type speech. However, if not everybody bought into a strategy or has the same concept of that strategy, it is not possible to execute. We will explore in future chapters how quiet leaders can best build a following around a plan (Chapter 7) and get people on the same page to execute (Chapter 5).

Executing

Ultimately, leaders and their organizations are graded on how they deliver and set up a system that facilitates these results. The quintessential picture of a results-driven organization is a charismatic, extraverted boss pounding the table and jettisoning hapless workers that do not meet standards, exhorting colleagues vociferously to just give a little bit more. It's debatable whether this is effective, but even if it is, a quiet leader's authentic style will be something other than this caricature. At times, it is necessary to push a team to the limits, and always a leader must create a sustainable system that achieves a high standard of excellence and drives accountability when things don't go as planned.

> *The quiet leader's dilemma*: Jim's company was in a neck-and-neck race to get its device out before a key competitor did the same. The stakes were high as the first one to the market would enjoy a variety of advantages—more media coverage, ability to be a first mover on pricing, first crack at locking in with key distributors, and the ability to bias the cardiologists that would use the device with preference and habits early before new products came into the marketplace. As Head of Product, Jim was accountable for the timeline; while his team had been putting in nights and weekends to try to meet the grade, he knew he was going to need more from them to meet their goal. As a quiet leader, Jim wondered whether his engineers would respond to his usual, soft-spoken, data-driven way of setting a goal, or whether he'd need to be more fired up. Further, as that was unnatural to him, would this be received well by his team? He had tried it before, and it felt both felt wrong and ineffective in reaching the team.

We will dive into the strengths of quiet leaders that can help Jim achieve what he needs to in setting goals, creating a system to achieve those goals, motivating his team, driving accountability, and moving forward when things don't exactly go as planned.

Once a leader has set a vision, built a system to execute that vision, communicating what's going on and why it's important is a crucial final piece that's key to leadership no matter who or what you're leading. Arguably, it's the most crucial aspect of leading: communication of vision and values with key constituents within and outside of the company is the one place that a leader can't easily delegate. For the purposes of examining the quiet leader's role in communicating, we'll break the practice down into two parts.

Connecting

Winning hearts and minds on a one-on-one basis. One aspect of building and growing an organization is winning key supporters to your cause whether they are investing their time, money, or platform in you. Doing this effectively is a key to being an effective leader.

> *The quiet leader's dilemma*: Massachusetts State Senator William Brownsberger's first career vision was not politics. However, out of a desire to serve his community and make a difference on issues that he cares about, he put his hat first into town politics and then state politics. Not naturally someone who liked grandstanding for large crowds, what sustained him was the one-on-one interactions he had each day with constituents and fellow lawmakers. With the realization that he was having these interactions in service of an important mission, he found these conversations ultimately the

most energizing part of his work, and (surprising as it was for him in hindsight) a source of balance when the other parts of the job were draining. Indeed, he found that his listening skills and ability to not be the loudest person in the room was effective; these deep individual relationships he has built over time enabled him to build consensus at the statehouse and beyond.

Having the volume of connections that leaders must to be effective requires forethought and bravery for quiet leaders as they require repeated social interaction; it's also important to note that, done right and authentically, many quiet leaders have found these interactions to be a source of great strength. Quiet leaders can be uniquely good at connecting given their ability to listen and observe. This gives them unique skill in understanding their counterpart's motivations, which in turn allows them to approach each interaction with mutual benefit in mind. We will examine how quiet leaders use their strengths and overcome their limitations to connect with others.

Building a following

Along with connecting with collaborators one on one, sometimes leaders have to broadcast their mission and vision on a larger scale. Winning converts to the cause on a larger scale is the realm extraverts are stereotypically known to inhabit comfortably. The stereotypical image is a Steve Ballmer pumping up his employees at a company meeting, sweat dripping off of his brow as he works the crowd into a frenzy. However, all leaders need to go beyond individual interactions such that an organization's mission resonates on a broader scale. Not everyone, though, is wired the same and will do this in the same authentic way.

The quiet leader's dilemma: Matt Johnson, a marketing agency founder and author on marketing strategies, felt he was at a crossroads as he was looking to build his business helping leaders market themselves and their organizations effectively. He had taken on multiple partnerships, was religiously posting on social media, and was doing all of the networking conferences he could to try to build a following for him and his work. A natural quiet leader, the energy he was pouring into these interactions that felt unnatural, and the relative lack of return on that investment he felt he was getting was unsustainable. He needed to find a different way forward if he was going to evangelize effectively but also sustainably.

Quiet leaders can also win hearts and minds and use different tools. Matt did find a way to thrive in his work promoting his business, and we will examine his and other ways that quiet leaders use preparation, a system, and focus on the mission to broadcast their mission, as well as tools available to us today in social media, videos, blogs, podcasts to complement what they do live.

What's Next?

We've covered the definition of a quiet leader, examined strengths and weaknesses, and created a framework for leadership we can use. As you consider these tasks, some self-reflection questions may be helpful as we move to the next section.

To put this into practice, we can revisit the questions to ask from Chapter 3.

- Which tasks of leadership do you practice the most in your role?
- Which ones are strengths?
- Which ones are most challenging for you as a quiet leader and why?
- What specific actions can you take over time to find your authentic way of practicing these tasks?

The Quiet Leader's Toolkit: Strategies We'll Revisit Throughout the Next Section

The next section gets practical, offering examples of how quiet leaders have navigated these key functions of leading in an authentic way, and covering frameworks to think about as you build your own authentic style. Some of the strategies are specific to each discipline; for example, speaking to a large group requires unique techniques and strategies relative to connecting in other settings. However, there are common themes that we'll keep coming back to that underpin how quiet leaders grow the depth and breadth of their impact. We call these the Quiet Leader's Toolkit. Tactics and practices that the successful quiet leaders that have contributed to this book have returned to often in their pursuit of performance.

The Quiet Leader's Toolkit

- **Preparation**
- **Transparency**
- **Collaboration**
- **Systematic Thinking**

Preparation

Whether you are preparing for a meeting with a counterparty, reading up on an expert source to build your view of the world, or rehearsing for a speech, preparation is a key aspect of how quiet leaders can get the most out of their strengths and overcome their limitations. While helpful for all leaders, preparation and the mental roadmap that preparation builds are uniquely useful for quiet leaders. First, this roadmap can help quiet leaders commit their message and their objectives to "muscle memory," so they can focus their energies on rising above key limitations like volume bias and leveraging their unique strengths. Second, quiet leaders often build their energy and conviction "inside-out"—preparation builds conviction, and conviction helps quiet leaders when it's important to practice the dimensions of leadership with clarity, emotion, and confidence. Finally, preparation helps with the efficiency of collaborative interaction, whether in a meeting filled with extraverts or in a key one-on-one meeting. We will explore across each element of leadership how quiet leaders can specifically prepare to be the most effective.

Transparency

Taking intention to be transparent and share more of yourself will come up often as we explore how to grow as quiet leaders. The core of many of the leadership disciplines we will cover is building trust with others; for quiet leaders, an approach is specifically useful given their tendency to process their thoughts and emotions internally and be perceived as aloof given their reserved demeanor. Along with transparency into who you are as a person, transparency into your thinking when you make decisions (the "why behind the what") is helpful to create buy-in and commitment. We will explore specifically for each discipline how that intention toward openness can build trust and help achieve your goals as a leader.

Collaboration

Leadership by nature is a people-intensive exercise. Collaborations with the people around you—trusted teammates, colleagues, and mentors—are a core part of growing quiet leadership across these key disciplines. Some examples of collaborations quiet leaders can use to be effective include seeking input of a mentor to navigate how to shine in an extraverted culture, leveraging the extraverts on your team to add a counterpoint to group discussions, and using the recommendation of a mutual colleague to build trust with a new contact before you even walk into a meeting. We will unpack how to best collaborate effectively to grow in all of the key aspects of leadership.

Systematic Thinking

As we'll go into in depth in Chapter 5, the ultimate job of a leader is to create a system around them (people, processes, and resources) that can accomplish the goals of the mission. The same goes for exercising your leadership as a quiet leader; we will dive into how to wire the work of connecting, broadcasting your mission, and understanding the world around you into your organization (with the caveat that some of these activities only you can undertake as the leader). Further, systems can wire action into improving your leadership practice—for example, committing to the calendar opportunities to get outside of your comfort zone and connect with others, or share your mission broadly in ways you haven't before. There are systematic ways to expand your presence in each of the key goals on the Quiet Leader's check list, and we will explore these in the coming chapters.

As we've established earlier in the book, not all quiet leaders are quiet in the same way. Some are quieter than others, and some might even be extraverts. There is no one-size-fits-all way to lead effectively as a quiet leader; however, there are tools to embrace your unique strengths to choose from, and other tools to overcome some natural limitations you may have. The key is picking what strategy works for you, trying it out, and going from there. Let's dive in.

Chapter 4

Setting a Direction

Understanding the world around you and using this information to set your strategy is the critical first step to enabling all of the other key activities of leadership. Like a foundation of a house, an accurate and detailed understanding of the world, and a plan for what you do about it underpins all of the other components of leadership.

First Step of Setting Direction: Building Understanding

If you have been effective at building understanding, you have built a detailed sense of the forces that shape your mission and how to influence them, and now have an opportunity to use this information to your advantage. For example, knowing the key individuals and institutions that shape your organization is critical to communicating your mission and vision to a larger audience. Even the smallest details can matter for your objectives. I once learned two important things from a conversation with a colleague: first, why a key prospective investor had declined to invest in them, and second, that the investor was a vegetarian. We were able to key in on why our products are different and ultimately win the day. Even better, we had this conversation at a restaurant that accounted for his dietary restrictions (I have been *that guy* who's taken a vegetarian to a steakhouse earlier in my career without that understanding).

- What is your "sector," or in other words, the community of organizations, people, and policies where your organization exists. For example, the sector of the companies my teams and I have built is biotechnology, and intersects with larger multinational corporations, federal agencies, advocacy groups, and the health care system.
- Who are your constituents (could be your customers as a revenue generating business, shareholders, collaborators, patients, or others)? What are their needs, and what drives them?
- In your sector, what are the organizations, forces, and people most likely to impact how you serve the needs of your different constituents? What drives them, and how can you influence them?
- On a macro level, what are the political, economic, and cultural developments in the world around you that will impact your ability to serve your constituents? How do you shape them?

If done right, building an understanding takes time and a process. We will focus here on how quiet leaders can best gather inputs, make sense of them, and create a strategic direction for the organization.

Gathering Inputs

As the questions demonstrate, understanding is an input driven exercise—the better the information you pull together, the deeper and more useful the worldview you develop as a consequence. Therefore, the information gathering component of understanding is critical to a leader's overall effectiveness. The questions that leaders are aiming to answer are seldom straightforward, and it is exceedingly rare that a single, reliable source can answer these. Understanding requires multiple sources of information, separating signal from the noise, and filling in the gaps in data that inevitably exist in trying to answer large scale qualitative questions.

A quiet leader has unique strengths when trying to gather such data. Quiet leaders are wired differently—research looking at brain activity in response to stimuli has shown that they are more focused on attending to internal thoughts and feelings and less to external stimuli.[28] This inward focus has helped many great quiet leaders to exercise their creativity in making sense of information, finding new sources of information, and shifting their worldview relative to the information they are seeing. Further, quiet leaders are better able to resist the tendency to skew a worldview based on limited data. Warren Buffett, Bill Gates, Mark Zuckerberg, and Albert Einstein are all successful, quiet individuals who created significant value for society by looking at problems and situations in unique and creative ways.

A quiet leader may have challenges when they must access important information through social interaction. Often, the most critical information doesn't exist on the web or in the literature—it may only exist in the experience of individuals. For example, academics, industry experts, consultants, and key customers might hold perspectives that can shape your worldview in a constructive way. In this way, quiet leaders'

---

[28] Laney, *The Introvert Advantage.*

limitations on how much social interaction is energizing can limit developing an understanding of the world that stays one step ahead of the competition. If you are not talking to key experts, chances are someone else will be, or that you will be missing critically important information.

I was one of these quiet leaders earlier in my career. I became adept at making the most out of the information I received and separating signal from noise. However, I was less comfortable with the types of one-on-one interactions necessary to fully round out a view of the world. Rather than lean into the discomfort and try to balance my quantitative analysis and reading with some informative conversations, I tried to convince myself these discussions weren't important. That worked for a while, but not when I was in charge because my team expected me to be able to use my position to learn things to benefit the organization. They knew instinctively that gathering this type of intelligence was better suited to senior leadership than finding other sources of information. Senior leaders can leverage their networks, reputation, and influence to get input that their teams can't. For example:

- An experienced leader may have former colleagues across the industry who can still share what's going on at other companies
- The leader of an organization is more likely to get reciprocity from a respected academic that's an expert in a key area because of the authority of the position
- A leader-to-leader conversation may be more candid and yield more mutually beneficial insight than one led by a subordinate.

I struggled, though, with how to actually do this. The idea of having several dozen conversations at a networking event, or calling half a dozen colleagues just to "catch up" seemed exhausting and a bit superficial to me. However, I have learned a great deal from friends and colleagues who can go one level deeper and learn about developments now and in the future through their many interactions among their network and their networking efforts.

Tom (the prototypical quiet leader we profiled earlier) in particular excels at building understanding despite his limitations. On the scale between introversion and extraversion, Tom is as much of an introvert as one can be. However, many of the unique insights and ideas he brings to our team come from what he calls his "friends in low places." In plain English, it is his deep network of scientists he has carefully built over a thirty-plus-year career and takes great care to maintain. Even though he abhors social interaction, he will make a point to travel to see his colleagues. Early on, I was always surprised and a little reluctant to approve some of his trips to far-flung places. I remember contemplating more than a few times how a bird-watching trip to Finland was a good investment for the company. However, over time, these were incredibly good investments. That birdwatching trip led to a collaboration that yielded one of Spero's candidate medicines that are now in human trials. To Tom, these visits aren't the same type of social interaction that exhausts him. He is having these interactions to further his mission, and at the very least, create a deeper friendship with his close colleagues. I've been a part of a few of these discussions that he's had over the years. Each time, I've marveled at how his discussions never have a specific agenda yet always arrive at some key insights that we could not have found elsewhere. For example, he's learned which company is developing a new drug, who is about to leave a particular university, and what new data might be coming at future medical conferences.

So how can a quiet leader add interpersonal interactions to the understanding they have of the world?

Leveraging Strengths: Getting the Most Out of Each Interaction in Understanding

Even if a quiet leader has fewer one-on-one interactions, their unique strengths can help squeeze every last drop of insight out of these discussions.

Signal to Noise

Many quiet leaders, including Tom, note that the silver lining of not naturally having as many one-on-one interactions is that they focus on quality interactions over quantity in learning about the world. Tom is selective about who he builds and maintains relationships with, which is out of necessity, given how draining interpersonal interaction can be for him. The benefit is that each of his interactions yield high value insights. He observes that his more extraverted colleagues have to work harder to separate what's true and actionable from what's not as they have a higher volume of interactions. There is value in preparation: proactively noting who in your universe is worth going deeper with and provides high-yield insights in order to focus on these individuals. Part of maintaining this discipline is not succumbing to fear of missing out—if you've determined that a particular interaction is very unlikely to build your worldview in a constructive way, it is perfectly fine to opt out. In fact, you're likely doing yourself a service as a quiet leader by preserving your focus for more productive activities.

Power of Listening and Asking

Quiet leaders by nature leave more space for others to share within conversations. Leaning into this tendency can offer quiet leaders opportunities to gain more knowledge about the world around them. As I typically don't dominate conversations, I tend to listen very carefully, not just to what my colleagues say, but also how they say it, and what they don't say. For at least the first five minutes of the meeting, I try not to say anything except for clarifying questions—statements such as "tell me more," or "I noticed that"—can make space for even deeper understanding.

Especially within an organization, a quiet leader's power to listen can be exquisitely beneficial for understanding. Junior (and sometimes even senior) members of a team have many incentives to agree with a leader. A leader who speaks more than they listen often will find that others within their organization say what they want to hear. You may think everything's going fine. It's what colleagues don't say and the casual asides they throw into conversations that can make the difference between diagnosing issues early and finding out about them when it's too late. At Spero, we call these asides "Easter eggs"—kind of like the bonus items in a video game, where probing further on those slightly passive-aggressive asides can enable a junior employee to tell you a problem exists when otherwise they might have been reluctant to come right out and say something.

Overcoming Limitations of Quiet Leaders to Build Understanding

Value of Preparation

Here's where the Quiet Leader's Toolkit comes into play; the power of preparation can be uniquely helpful in building understanding. Quiet leaders who have thought ahead of time about what they'd like to learn can guide conversations to get the most out of each interaction. Before high-value interactions, I will typically answer three questions for myself in writing:

- What is the person's background?
- What am I looking to learn from their experiences?
- What can I offer in return to help build the relationship?

The last question is an important one not to overlook. Since I am not doing as much of the talking, I also lean on my follow-ups to be as helpful as my colleagues are to me. For example, if my colleague had mentioned wanting to know about a particular topic, I might send them an article or connect them with someone with expertise.

Power of Giving

Being known as someone that has and can share unique insights is an important way for quiet leaders to stay current. Cultivating one's expertise and being known as someone willing to share insight can have the effect of having others in your community seek you out. This is especially helpful for quiet leaders who are exhausted by the idea of frequent networking and seeking out one-on-one conversations that may not have an immediate purpose but deepen relationships and allow for sharing of information. There are multiple ways to do this—the written word, speeches, and a social medial presence can all establish one as an expert and facilitate the "game coming to you."

Mission-Driven Activities

Along with one's reputation, another way to have the "game come to you" is to organize interaction around a common mission. For example, organizing a group of peers around a particular issue of interest can create the type of interpersonal exchange of ideas that quiet leaders need.

Working on a group task or mission is often an easier hurdle to cross than a set of unrelated one-on-one interactions or a networking event. Carl, a technology marketing executive, took the opportunity to create his own subgroup within a larger conference to explore a regulatory issue that would impact one of his key products. By finding like-minded people and organizing the topics, he was able to build relationships and expand his understanding in a way more authentic to him than finding some of these experts at the conference one-on-one and striking up a conversation. For quiet leaders aspiring to create their own mission driven activities—a few suggestions:

- Choose a topic that you are confident about—Carl notes that his reticence around interpersonal interaction fades when the topic is one that he's passionate about. As such, he's chosen his activities accordingly
- Aim to be no more than the second most qualified person in the group you convene. When deeper experts than you are join your gathering, you are adding value to your attendees and also building your network. Further, for quiet leaders that don't like being the center of attention, having bigger stars around you ensures that the focus is on the content and not on you.

Power of Format

Quiet leaders can maximize their efforts generating insight by choosing the format that works best for them. If one-on-one discussions or cocktail parties are draining, other venues like Zoom, FaceTime, or phone calls can work. An active presence on social media can create the kind of thought leadership that makes it easier to have interactions that form a view of the world. Rahul, a CEO of a growing organization supporting clinical trials, has leaned into podcasts as a way to build relationships with senior leaders in his industry. The podcasts create an opportunity to build relationships, focus the conversation on questions that are of interest to him and the audience, and do so in a format that feels more natural and mission-focused than a series of one-on-one discussions. As another example, Luke, a journalist, has used his online publication as a medium to engage senior leaders and provide them with a space to write about topics of relevance to them. Some degree of preparation can help here—knowing what you want to learn, extending this to who might teach it to you, and mapping out ways that you might reach them in the format that works best for you can fill in the gaps for a quiet leader.

Motivating Yourself to Have More Interactions—Power of Systematic Thinking

The systems mindset we reviewed in Chapter 3 can be helpful in building understanding. For example, Tom finds great practical value in a systematic approach to interactions with his trusted colleagues that ensures that he is staying in close touch with them. Each year, he commits to travel to their cities to have dinner, or coffee, or undertake whatever hobby is their passion. In addition, he makes time to speak with them over the phone several times a year.

So how can you use structure to maximize the "understanding" interactions you have? While many of the above strategies create alternatives to the type of interaction-intensive activities that can build your view of the world, there is sometimes no substitute for getting "out there" and meeting your collaborators. To complement the non-interactive ways that a quiet leader can build signal (collaboration, different formats, becoming a sought-out source), a bit of structure can help reinforce the need to have collaborative interactions. For example, putting on the schedule at regular intervals a reminder to call a new or old colleague, or to join a networking event can make it easier. When you do get there, pace yourself. Doing enough that feels authentic is better than overdoing it and not giving your best to each interaction.

Leveraging Colleagues and Coworkers

The power of collaboration we reviewed from the Quiet Leader's Toolkit can also help. Your teammates have different degrees of skill in the learning about the world around them, and different relationships that complement each other. A quiet leader does not have to have all of the key insights to build a worldview—he or she just needs access to them. Transparency into your strategy and goals for learning about the world is critical here. Incorporating this mindset into the company culture can pay big dividends. At our company, we reduce this to practice using the calendar, periodically having a strategy session where a first step is to learn about the world around us and how it has changed since the last time we discussed the strategy. Further, we have a culture of sharing some of these key conversations at our team meetings and through notes. These currents of conversations that flow between our team help us all build a deeper worldview than we could have had otherwise, whether or not we enjoy the types of network-based discussions that build them.

Second Step of Setting Direction: Build a Plan Based on Your Understanding

Now that you have gathered some unique insights from some easy and some hard to access sources, what do you do about it?

Making Sense of It All: Importance of Process in Setting a Course of Action

Once you've gathered the necessary input, it takes time, thought, and iteration to form a worldview. Quiet leaders that we have spoken to highlight that their process to get to this cogent worldview is very different from their extraverted colleagues—while extraverts often build their worldview in group discussion, debate, and repeating this process over time, quiet leaders and especially introverted ones need individual time for reflection before they "come up for air" and begin to share their views with a small group.

Structuring this is important—if you don't build in time to reflect and create based on what you've learned, something else that seems more pressing will take its place. Further, getting pulled into the extraverted style of ideation may not be productive or energizing for a quiet leader. Finally, especially if you are a senior leader, despite your tendency to think deep thoughts by yourself, sharing what you've learned is important. At Spero and other companies I have helped build, we schedule debriefs on what we learned from major events—medical conferences, investor meetings—a few days after the event to give quiet leaders time to synthesize and share what's important without the pressure of batting around individual observations before they have a chance to reflect. Further, the extraverts on the team need group time beforehand to begin to form their impressions, and we leave space for this as well.

Particular Mind Traps in Setting Direction for Quiet Leaders to Avoid

As you make sense of what you have learned about the world in which you lead, quiet leaders that have been a part of this book have noted a few important mind traps in translating understanding to direction.

- **Charisma trap**: As you have the types of conversations that build your worldview, some opinion leaders make their points more vociferously and memorably than others. There is a danger in over-emphasizing these viewpoints even if they are no more well informed than those delivered less colorfully. Social science research supports the risk of this mind trap: in a study looking at organizational behavior, organizations were found to be more likely to emulate practices from competitors with charismatic leaders whether or not those practices were more effective.[29] In my own experience, we often speak to medical experts as we think about the market viability of our medicines. One particular expert is known for aiming to be controversial, and for speaking in "headline worthy" phrases. In general, if possible, I try to speak with him last so as not to overly bias the overall hypotheses I am forming from these discussions.

- **Data trap:** Quiet leaders by nature tend to be more comfortable with data, literature, and otherwise less people intensive resources to learn about the world than with one-on-one conversations. There is a danger, then, to over-emphasize the ideas within articles, blogs, social media over direct sources such as discussions with experts within or outside of your team. Sometimes, depending on the question at hand, a key conversation with an expert may outweigh all of the third-party articles you read (the reverse can also be true depending on the question). A few questions can help tease apart what's the right balance:

  o Can the question be answered quantitatively and definitively (for example whether one sales force performs better than another in a given territory), or is the answer more qualitative (which product offerings are most likely to compete effectively with a peer firm's)?

  o Is the issue at hand simple (clear problem, clear solution like a missing part in a machine) or subject to multiple unpredictable factors (stock performance over time)?

---

[29] "Firms Tend to Imitate Competitors Led by Charismatic-Not Narcissistic-CEOS," Foster School of Business, 2018, https://foster.uw.edu/research-brief/firms-tend-imitate-competitors-led-charismatic-not-narcissistic-ceos/.

If you are choosing the second option for most questions, you are not alone. Most topics you will address as a leader are neither simple nor easy to answer solely with data. In these cases, setting direction can't just rely on quantitative analysis or what you've researched on an issue. The ability to benefit from individuals' "gut feel" on complex issues will be important as well. The Cynefin framework from Snowden and Boone in the *Harvard Business Review* examines how teams made decisions in a variety of complex settings; a common thread was taking the opportunity to hear a variety of voices and their interpretation of a multifactorial situation before setting a direction.[30]

- **Expertise trap**: Sometimes, the world around which you're trying to set direction is one that you think you know well. As a quiet leader, it sometimes feels far easier to rely on your own expertise than doing the hard and sometimes uncomfortable work of seeking outside input. Your own expertise is no doubt useful, and might even be an important reason why you got the role in the first place. That said, given the complexity of setting direction in most contexts, having some humility about that expertise can be important. Your particular situation may or may not match your prior experience. Particularly in fast moving fields, your view may not even be current. Further, if you as the leader place undue emphasis on your own expertise, you are also missing an opportunity to cultivate that expertise around your organization. For a variety of reasons, engaging with others to complement your own expertise can result in higher quality decisions. One strategy teams use to avoid the expertise trap is

---

[30] David J. Snowden and Mary Boone, "A Leader's Framework for Decision Making," *Harvard Business Review*, December 7, 2015, https://hbr.org/2007/11/a-leaders-framework-for-decision-making.

to have someone in a debrief take the contrarian point of view in order to pressure test the logical support for a decision.

What's Next After You've Made Sense of it All and Set Direction?

So now that you've used your strengths and overcome your limitations as a quiet leader to form your worldview and killer plan, two critical tasks await you. A first step is building consensus among your team and key constituents. Second, and perhaps even more important, is actually getting the plan in motion. We dive into both key tasks in the coming chapters.

Chapter 5

Executing—Designing the Organization to Get Things Done

So, you've formed a view of the world, and you've used it to come up with a plan to do something about it. Plans are a critical part of leadership, but you will be judged by how your organization executes them. For clarity, a leader's contribution to execution isn't the tactical work that the organization accomplishes. Even though leaders, especially at smaller organizations, may undertake many tasks to get the job done, these can be delegated to others. The key activity that only a leader can undertake is building and maintaining the "system" by which your organization accomplishes its goals. This is relevant if you are within a one hundred-thousand-person organization or an army of one.

We focus on a few core elements of designing your organization to execute. These are particularly relevant to quiet leaders as they will approach them very differently from extraverts:

- **Building your team**—An effective team with the right skills and personalities is a core element of great execution

- **Creating effective team dynamics**—Once you have your A-team, getting them to work together optimally is just as critical as having the right people
- **Communicating Objectives and Accountability**—Once your team and how it works is set up, the core of getting things done is defining what's important, measuring what gets done, and taking action based on what you measure

Building the Team

Crucial to many leaders' plans is the need to scale an organization; scale requires people, and putting them together in a way that can realize the vision that you have collectively. Hiring is one of the most critical decisions any leader can make; great hires increase the chances that bad decisions can turn out right, and poor hires can make the right strategy seem wrong.

At Spero, while our vision to make life better for patients suffering from infection is the right one, how we initially planned to get there back when we started was wrong. We picked the wrong medicines to develop in the wrong sector of the market to grow; however, the team we built, the specialized expertise they have, and the intellectually humble dynamic we fostered led us to some hard data-driven questions about where we were headed a few years into our journey, as well inspired some side projects that ended up being more attractive than our original plan.

What must quiet leaders consider when building a team? In this chapter, we will focus on the architecture of the team for quiet leaders—how to construct teams and how to identify the right fit for you and for the organization. Once you have found the right fit for your team, your candidates will evaluate whether to invest their time and livelihood with you. We will cover best practices on how to win converts to your mission and vision in the coming chapters.

What is the right team structure for a quiet leader? It is often far easier for a quiet leader to gravitate toward other quiet leaders. In many ways, you speak the same language (at the same volume), and do not need the same level of external affirmation from each other that an extravert might need. Teams can benefit from quiet leaders' propensity to listen and leave space for others, think carefully and then communicate a plan, leverage their capacity for self-reflection, and their tendency to moderate their reactions to either triumph or adversity. Further, quiet leaders' tendency to process internally and then share more fully baked thoughts can resonate with other quiet leaders who are used to this style of formulating ideas.

Does this mean the best teams are 100 percent composed of quiet leaders? No. A mix of quiet leaders and extraverts can yield a better decision-making dynamic. Leadership researchers have examined this phenomenon called *dominance complementarity*.[31] Consistently, studies have shown that a team balanced across personality traits yields better team cohesion and results than teams with less balance. This phenomenon has practical roots. Quiet leaders' tendency to think, then act can have great value. Extraverts' ability to push a conversation, bring new data to a discussion that's facilitated by their interest in connecting with others, and tip the balance between action and deliberation can influence a team dynamic in a healthy way. This is even true beyond quiet leaders. Aoife, who leads a public company in the life sciences, notes that that she, as an extravert, values the extraverts on her team as their ability to engage her in real time brainstorming and push back on her when necessary. Doing this real time creates permission for the team's introverts to

---

[31] Francesca Gino, "Introverts, Extroverts, and the Complexities of Team Dynamics," *Harvard Business Review*, August 12, 2015, https://hbr.org/2015/03/introverts-extroverts-and-the-complexities-of-team-dynamics?registration=success.

do the same, even if they are more reticent at first. This leads to a better decision at the end of the brainstorming process.

In addition, certain functions tend to be populated by extraverts (sales, external facing roles—though not always). Having a bias toward quiet leaders limits who you might choose from for these key functions. There is also value in having extraverts on the team that prefer specific outward facing activities, such as networking, that quiet leaders need more intention to do at scale. A coordinated approach to sharing a company's mission can greatly expand an organization's reach and overall effectiveness (more on this in later chapters).

Is there a right mix of quiet leaders versus extraverts on your team? No one size fits all, and it certainly depends on the tasks at hand. Note that the appropriate mix of extraversion versus introversion also depends on the mission of your organization. You will adjust the mix of your team based on how much external interaction is required (for example an event-planning firm versus a think tank). Further, the bias to action that senior leadership requires (a crisis management firm versus a firm focused on long-term strategic planning) may also shift the optimal personality mix. I certainly saw this during medical training, noticing that the action-packed Emergency Department both attracted and preferred extraverts throughout their ranks (they had their hands full with me during my rotation), while professions like neurology and internal medicine that took time to contemplate a diagnosis tended to have more quiet leaders among their ranks. This all said, even if your group trends more extraverted (or quieter) for the task at hand, the point is that a mix of personalities is still optimal.

So, if working with quiet leaders can feel comfortable, but may not be the best thing for the team, how do you recruit extraverts as a quiet leader? Having a conscious understanding of your tendency to more immediately connect with quiet leaders is a good first step. In effect, personality diversity is another critical element of diversity to plan for (along with racial, gender, and other strata of diversity) in building a workforce. The next step is constructing the process to encourage this type of diversity. We've used a team-oriented process for hiring at the companies I have led. Along with being consistent with our company culture, our experience suggests group hiring leads to better decisions. Management research backs this up. For example, when Google tracked the performance of new hires over time, the collective ratings of the group were a better predictor of that performance than any individual, even if that individual was a leader or a founder.[32]

The Quiet Leader's Toolkit comes in handy here. The power of collaboration and systematic thinking can help find the right personality balance on the team. Leaders can enlist their teammates in a way that accounts for potential inherent personality bias they might bring to the table. For example, ensuring that the interview includes extraverts can help with a balanced process. In addition, as a quiet leader getting to know an extraverted candidate, stating upfront that you are a quiet leader can put a more extraverted candidate at ease. They will understand why you may not as readily reflect back their energy as much as they might have expected. When I interview candidates, especially extraverted ones, I will state that sometimes people find me hard to read, that I am being direct with them in turn. The context helps the extravert, and the directness lets them know where they stand even though I give fewer non-verbal signals. Another process point many quiet leaders have mentioned, especially for more senior hires, is the importance of non-interview interactions such as dinners, and (if appropriate) presentations to the interview panel. These maximize the chance that you can see who a candidate really is beyond a structured interview setting where one can rehearse.

---

[32] Atta Tarki, "How to Avoid Groupthink When Hiring," *Harvard Business Review*, August 13, 2019, https://hbr.org/2019/08/how-to-avoid-groupthink-when-hiring.

Finally, for quiet leaders, references make a huge difference in calibrating impressions of an extravert. Corroborating data can lead you away from biases formed through a single (or even a few) interactions. For example, candidates may be on their best behavior, or may be presenting in an introverted way toward which you are inherently biased. For the key position of Investor Relations (the individual who sets our strategy for communicating with Wall Street), we had two candidates at Spero, one a quiet leader and one an extravert. I was dead set against the extravert since he seemed to be "too much" relative to the quiet candidate who came across as thoughtful and prepared. I wasn't sure I was ready for the energy the extravert brought to our interactions. I felt that I had a much clearer picture of who the introvert candidate was and how I might collaborate with him.

However, with extraverts on the interview panel and with the benefit of references, I began to see the extraverted candidate in a different light. Approaching references as a quiet leader (unsurprisingly) involves listening and observing a lot more than it does directing the reference. In fact, you can learn something about how much they like a candidate from the first correspondence onward:

- How quickly do they get back to me?
- Are they enthusiastic in their correspondence?
- Do they use any qualifying phrases?
- How much do they speak—sometimes references who are trying to tiptoe around a candidate they like but don't love will over-explain.

His references were extremely specific about the great things he had brought to their organizations, and they went out of their way to speak to us and put in a good word. The comparison between the enthusiasm his references offered and the other candidate's references was clear, which suggested that the extraverted candidate was someone special. I pieced together that his nervousness at meeting me drove his energy in our initial interactions. We hired the extravert based on the group process. In hindsight, it was the right call as was setting up a process designed to get past our inherent tendency to hire people just like us.

Running the Team

Once you have hired a mix of quiet leaders and introverts, running the team has its own considerations specifically for quiet leaders. Working with a mixed group of quiet leaders and extraverts requires tailoring our approaches to each member to build the deepest working relationship possible.

> Polly, a quiet leader with a large multifunctional team to manage, found that engaging with her full team which included many extraverts proved to be draining and less productive when it came to deep thought and brainstorming. She learned that it was better for her to engage with a smaller group of her quiet leaders when she wanted to brainstorm and formulate, and then with her larger group following that. Being up-front with her team about her tendency to do this helped address the concerns of extraverts that felt left out of the initial process.

What extraverts need from quiet leaders: Extraverts think out loud, derive energy from their interactions, and often need more interaction from their collaborators to trust the feedback they are receiving. Further, many extraverts see the quantity of interaction between mentor/mentee as a mark of their importance much more so than their quieter colleagues. From a quiet leader's perspective, finding a balance between meeting these needs, remaining authentic, and ensuring you are devoting equal energy to quieter colleagues requires careful thought and needs retuning over time.

Finding this balance often requires quiet leaders to be creative and get out of their comfort zone to give extraverts the feedback that they need. The concept of openness and vulnerability from the Quiet Leader's Toolkit can be helpful here. Tim is a longtime leader of scientific organizations and a quiet leader by nature. He notes that for quiet leaders, it is sometimes both difficult and unproductive to maintain a certain affect in engaging with his extraverted team. Extraverts in particular can see through inauthenticity. He instead has found that employing directness with his extraverted colleagues can be very effective. With these colleagues, he is mindful to vocalize what he is thinking even when sometimes his natural tendency is to internalize some of these thoughts. Further, he's learned that teammates of different personality types need different intensity of feedback to register the same response. A very direct statement may sound like a megaphone to his quiet colleagues. In contrast, his extraverted colleagues need a more direct, intensive statement to hear the same gravity and magnitude of the message. As some extraverts can find quiet leaders hard to read, this strategy (executed with respect and tact of course) can eliminate some of the guesswork as extraverts will feel they know where they stand even if they can't always read a quiet leader's body language.

As with connecting with others, the medium in which a quiet leader engages with his or her team can also make a difference. In this post-pandemic hybrid environment, there are many choices a leader can make on how they can engage—live, via video, on the phone, scheduled, or "drop-ins," for example. I've learned to tailor my approach based on personality type. Quiet leaders on my team prefer structure: a set time, an agenda sent ahead of time, key questions sent over email with some time to reflect, and a balance between virtual and in person. This reflects quiet leaders' need for solitude to gain energy and their desire to be prepared and think things through before sharing ideas. If (and there often are) reasons to engage your quieter colleagues upfront, using text or chat functions can help create brief time and space for quiet leaders to reflect and come back with thoughtful answers. Extraverts benefit from a broader mix—meetings in person, drop ins to their office. Unscheduled interactions are welcome and accrue to many extraverts' values on quantity (as well as quality) of interaction. Long emails that may work well for quiet leaders may not be as well received by extraverts, who prefer to talk things out.[33]

Aoife, the CEO, creates formats that appeal to both extraverts and quiet leaders to drive consensus for big decisions. She writes a memo that her team can review ahead of time, discusses the memo at an in-person meeting for the extraverts on the team, and then allows a week to pass such that all have had a chance to formulate their thoughts and any objections. Others, such as senior management teams at Amazon, have also used memos even more frequently as a way to cultivate deep thought and level the playing field between team members with different propensities to vocalize their thoughts.[34]

In fact, for quiet leaders that do much of their processing internally before sharing with the team, the lack of "kicking things around" can take some adjustment from extraverts. Extraverts can feel a quiet leader doesn't value them if they are not in the room when a decision is

---

[33] Liz Fosslien and Mollie West, "Communication Tips for Introverts and Extroverts, from Two of Your Favorite Authors," https://www.quietrev.com/communication-tips-for-introverts-and-extroverts-from-two-of-your-favorite-authors/.

[34] Justin Bariso, "Why Intelligent Minds Like Jeff Bezos Embrace the Rule of Writing," Inc., https://www.inc.com/justin-bariso/how-to-write-amazon-jeff-bezos-memos-meetings-clear-writing-clear-thinking-rule-of-writing.html.

formulated. Quiet leaders can avoid this mismatch of expectations by being open and upfront about how they think and formulate decisions (as Polly did with her team), but also by meeting their extraverted team members partway. The power of systematic thinking can help. For example, committing to the calendar times to drop in and brainstorm with extraverted colleagues can help these colleagues feel valued. In addition, identifying specific issues or tasks where extraverts can be involved in a decision from start to finish will increase buy-in even if a quiet leader's tendency is to move toward a decision with quiet internal reflection or a smaller group.

Engaging with extraverts can also make the quality of decisions and creative thinking better. There is often value in the extravert method of idea refinement. Done to a degree that's comfortable, a quiet leader may build on their ideas as well as get better buy-in for decisions. I have often found that I walk out of a session with an extravert with some new ideas (and admittedly, some ideas I need to deprioritize as well). As with any tendency that doesn't come naturally to a quiet leader, reducing this to practice by quantifying and scheduling how often you want to engage in this can find the right balance.

Complex decisions benefit from consulting an experienced team's opinions before making a final call. There is considerable evidence that the composite of multiple opinions when things aren't clear provides a better outcome (see Snowden and Boone's Cynefin framework that we refer to earlier in the book for a good explanation).[35] Employing this philosophy as a quiet leader requires sorting through the differences in how quiet leaders and extraverts make their points.

This is a multivariable equation—opinions on complex topics each have their own logic, specific motivations, and level of conviction. Of these, conviction manifests very differently between quiet leaders and extraverts. Extraverts may, other things equal, speak loudly and articulately

---

[35] Snowden and Boone, "A Leader's Framework."

about all of their opinions. However, this does not necessarily mean they hold those opinions any more strongly than their quieter colleagues. John, a quiet leader, venture capitalist, and former CEO, notes that he looks for "conviction tells" when hearing different opinions from a group that he needs to synthesize. For example, does an extravert back off of an opinion when presented with a cogent counter argument? Does a quiet leader's body language change as an opinion is debated? After the discussion, does the quiet leader come back to emphasize a point or add more evidence to the argument (which often means he or she didn't agree with the consensus in the first place). One member of my team is a very quiet (but very effective leader); I know when I've reached his bedrock based on body language and based on phrases he chooses (such as, you could do that, but it may not work out the way you want....).

Once you've made an estimation of the different opinions around a complex decision, realizing that extraverts and quiet leaders require different amounts of time to reflect and contemplate is an important part of achieving buy-in for a decision. The speed to incorporation of a complex decision is not necessarily directly correlated to extraversion. Some quiet leaders on our team come to an answer fairly quickly, and some extraverts need time to deliberate. For this reason, we institute the "twenty-four-hour rule" for complicated decisions. This gives more contemplative individuals time to incorporate the facts, ask for clarification, and helps avoid revisiting decisions in the future when you've moved faster with a decision than its understanding.

Both preparation and systematic thinking factor into running your team optimally as a quiet leader. Onboarding is an incredible opportunity as a quiet leader to prepare in advance to run your team. Being systematic, and learning upfront about how you process information, how you prefer to interact, and how your team member does the same will give you a head start in tailoring your approach to your team optimally.

Communicating Objectives

A clear understanding of what needs to be accomplished is an important first step in executing. Quiet leaders will communicate what's important differently. For example, my natural preference, like many quiet leaders, is to have important discussions such as our objectives for the year one-to-one rather than in a group setting. The downside of doing this too much, is the risk that different individuals may hear different things. For a set of common objectives, this can be at best confusing and at worst mean a team is not executing optimally as they have all interpreted what you have said differently.

Some practical suggestions may help a quiet leader bridge their comfort with discussing something important in a small group with the need to make sure all are on same page.

- **Complement an all-hands discussion with a hybrid approach**: A hybrid of an external presentation, written materials, and then a one-on-one follow-up can help balance sharing common information and delivering it with some personal emphasis. It can also be a style more comfortable to a quiet leader. For example, this could mean using a broadcast medium like video or an all-hands meeting to make sure all employees have heard the same thing from the quiet leader at least once. Further, to emphasize the personal discussion that comes more naturally to quiet leaders, it could mean following up in smaller groups using identical source material. These sessions can be particularly useful to focus on how the broader message specifically applies to the smaller group and their specific roles in the organization.
- **Using systematic thinking**: Using the Quiet Leader's Toolkit to build communication into the system can also help get people on the same page. At several companies I've been a part of, we

empower a group of senior employees to take our initial suggestions on goals, and put their stamp on them. This group also has the objective of communicating these goals in more depth to those around them—their reports and their peers. For a quiet leader, involving others in a process commits them to the goal, builds awareness, and requires less volume from the quiet leader to drive this across in their presentations.

Accountability

Once the strategy is set and roles are clear, a critical part of execution is ensuring that all team members are accountable to them. This can be one of the most difficult aspects of being a quiet leader. External expectations of what leaders do to keep teams accountable don't square with their authentic style. Quiet leaders are less prone to big speeches when things are going well, or tirades when things aren't. How can quiet leaders show up in a way that's authentic but that works?

Many of the quiet leaders that contributed to this book speak to the power of creating a system of accountability and letting that system do the work instead of relying on the efforts of the quiet leader or any one individual. Putting the best of these systems together:

- **Measure, measure, measure**—With a well-thought-through framework around performance, quiet leaders can use the system rather than having to be the loudest voice in the room. First, the data becomes the focus rather than the individual, and it speaks for itself. Second, these quantitative measures, tracked over time, invite hypotheses on how to improve on poor performance and maintain good performance. Thirdly, the numbers invite some degree of transparency that can motivate others. Finally, if the measurables are chosen right, the system can incentivize reaching for the stars as what's expected is quantified, and can serve as its own reinforcement if your team wants to go above and beyond.

The first step of creating a system of accountability that speaks for itself is figuring what to measure and how to measure it. Examples of measurables include revenues, timelines (delivering a clinical study or product with a baseline level of quality on time), quantification of elements that matter to your customers (e.g., customer satisfaction metrics), or inputs (number of publications, number of meetings, percentage of households visited for a political campaign) when outputs are subject to variables beyond the team's control. This requires careful thought—what you measure is what your team will do. I often use balancing metrics to ensure that we don't hit the goal at the expense of other, harder-to-measure elements that also matter. For example, the timeliness of key deliverables for medicines matters, but the system also has metrics for quality (like quality of clinical data) to avoid the temptation to cut corners.

- **Communicate these measures and check in on a set schedule well ahead of key deliverables**—It doesn't help if you check in on measurables for the first time days before a deliverable. Checking in at periodic intervals allows for course corrections over time while they can still be relevant to overall objectives. Further, the cadence takes some of the drama out of the final review as it happens at regular intervals. Systematic thinking is very helpful; at the companies I have worked at, we ask the team to create a monthly (or bimonthly depending on the deliverable) one-page tracker for key measurables. Their progress and any optimization necessary are transparent for all and is its own motivator for people without the need to use the force of personality.

- **Emphasize rewarding good performance**—Significant literature suggests that positive reinforcement is a preferable motivator to negative reinforcement. Studies have correlated an increased use of positive incentives over negative reinforcement with higher performance and lower turnover.[36,37] This is true especially when creativity and teamwork are required for the tasks at hand, as negative reinforcement arouses the parts of the brain that shut down creative thought. In this sense, using the system to highlight positive behavior on a consistent basis keeps the team focused on the task at hand, leaves more room for creativity, and exemplifies more of what you want as a leader. Inspiring fear of punishment may be the traditional conception of a powerful and effective leader. However, that approach doesn't do much to incentivize creativity, free flow of information, and building a place where your most talented employees want to stick around. Further, a quiet leader who may be perceived as hard to read and aloof can inadvertently amplify this misperception when they use negative reinforcement relative to a more extraverted leader whose more natural interactions with a team can balance this out.

Independent of quiet leadership, different leaders exhibit different levels of stinginess with praise and compliments. Especially as a quiet leader who does not get animated, I take great intention in using nonverbal media to praise the team. After major

---

[36] Steven J. Condly, Richard E. Clark, Harold D. Stolovitch, "The Effects of Incentives on Workplace Performance: A Meta-Analytic Review of Research Studies," *Performance Improvement Quarterly* 16, no. 3 (2003): pp. 46–63, https://eric.ed.gov/?id=EJ957565.

[37] Chester Elton and Adrian Gostick, *The Carrot Principle: How the Best Managers Use Recognition to Engage Their People, Retain Talent, and Accelerate Performance,* (New York, NY: Free Press, 2007). https://books.google.com/books/about/The_Carrot_Principle.html?id=e_Tb1aso78sC.

accomplishments, I use video or email to ensure that we have given credit where it is due to add to what I do in person, as many (particularly extraverts) mistake my usual even-keel as a lack of enthusiasm for a milestone. As an example, after a major clinical study came in positive, I found myself having to reaffirm to the team that I saw nothing wrong with the data, given my relatively muted reaction to fabulous news. To combat this, I often empower others (such as the leader of a project) to take the limelight and deliver positive reinforcement since it's both motivating for others to get the limelight; they are often better than I am at conveying the sincere emotion behind a major milestone.

- **Asking your team to go above and beyond**—One fear I have had as I've grown as a quiet leader is how I might really get my team into a new gear for a critical deadline or an emergent event that requires a rapid response. This is the time when the "win one for the Gipper" speeches are usually given in the movies and in popular lore about strong and successful leaders. I couldn't give one if I tried. The reality, in my experience, is that these speeches might feel good in the moment, but they do very little; if you've hired the right team that cares about the mission, put them in a system that rewards success and identifies areas to improve, and have planned for contingencies, teams will rise to the occasion. It does pay to appreciate the effort when your team does it (see above for positive reinforcement).

Dealing with Setbacks

Sometimes, things don't go according to plan. This is where a quiet leader can truly shine. Teams look to the leader for how they should react. A quiet leader has some natural gifts that can help keep the team focused. They tend to be less emotive and react internally rather than externally, which is a major asset when a calm approach to a problem is what's needed. Taken too far, a quiet leader's natural tendency to turn inward can be a limitation to overcome. Teams need to hear from you, even if what you'd rather do is go in a quiet room and sort things out in your mind. Keeping in mind some specifics can help a quiet leader remember how to address the troops when things aren't going as planned.

- **Explain what happened**—Restating the issue and making sense of it is an important first step; your team will be independently trying to make sense out of a major setback. The more complex the setback, the more room for differential interpretations, and therefore, differential ideas on where to move forward. Setting the tone on how to view a problem can help with the unity of purpose for a solution. When one of the companies we have worked with had a medicine that we decided to shelve for further development, we brought the team in charge of the medicine into a detailed session to explain why to key members of the team. That understanding helped generate creative suggestions from the team on how to move forward.

- **Acknowledge what you know, what you don't know, and how you aim to find out**—During the start of the pandemic, many leaders had to make major shifts to their business seemingly overnight. In complex crisis situations, more often than not information is unclear. Acknowledging this uncertainty builds the credibility you need with your team as events unfold and can invite them to be a part of figuring out what's going on. The CEO of Marriott Corporation took the time to make a video for Marriott's thousands of employees that went into what was going on with the pandemic and the impact on the business. What was telling and why the video went viral even beyond Marriott was the humility the CEO showed in acknowledging what he didn't know and how he'd work with his team to find out.

- **Acknowledge what you and others are feeling**—Although there may be many pressing tasks during a crisis, taking a moment to acknowledge the gravity and emotion of a situation is incredibly useful so you can get back to fixing the problem. Especially if you have a team of quiet leaders, doing more on acknowledging what the team must feel is actually a good thing since quiet leaders won't always make their emotions visible externally. Even if you observe that your team is unperturbed, the quiet leaders especially might be dealing with a torrent of emotions internally. It is good practice whether you feel your team has been affected or not to access those emotions upfront.

With the team focused after taking these steps, you can then start to task key leaders with moving forward. Tasking them with finding out what you don't know and acting on what you do know is what comes next, but only after you've set the stage as a leader with the prior steps.

Shifting Gears

Chapter 5 covered the nuts and bolts of getting things done through your organization as a leader. Now, the next chapters shift gears to how quiet leaders can take their vision and what they've executed with their team and share it with individuals and larger groups. Further, we will go into how quiet leaders can build connections with individuals and groups to drive the mission forward beyond what the team is already doing. This is key to growth and to securing the interest, resources, and people necessary to keep driving your plans.

Chapter 6

Connecting—How Quiet Leaders Can Build Trust and Advance Mutually Beneficial Collaborations

Relative to the stereotypical elected official, Senator Will Browns-berger is a rare bird in the Massachusetts statehouse—he is not the loudest person in the room. He believes the secret to being effective as a State Senator re-elected multiple times is the depth of relationships he has built with his colleagues and his constituents. He does not see his effectiveness as linked to how he moves the crowd, but how he gets things done for his district one person at a time—either with one colleague in the statehouse, or with a constituent.

Whether you're leading a small startup or a Fortune 500 Corporation, forming an authentic connection with your collaborator is a critical part of doing the job. You may be convincing your first investor to commit to a financing, a star employee to join the company, or a reluctant leader of a community group to lend their voice to your cause. The daily work of leadership is building relationships and collaborating through them to get your mission accomplished. Quiet leaders will bring unique strengths to this important task and unique limitations. Let's dive into them and how quiet leaders can be effective.

The Objectives of Interpersonal Connection

We'll take a practical approach to connecting, with an emphasis on where quiet leaders can focus to be most effective.

- *Building trust*—This is where Senator Brownsberger focused his energies to become effective as a quiet leader: convincing your counterpart that you are a reasonable actor that will be faithful to your mutually shared objectives. This is the basic foundation of all interpersonal relationships. Quiet leaders have strengths that support building trust given their listening skills, their (at least overt) ability to stay calm in a variety of situations, and a natural tendency to invest more deeply in fewer relationships versus more superficially in a larger set of connections. On the converse side, quiet leaders who are not well known yet to their counterparts can seem aloof, reserved, and can invite assumptions (conceit, arrogance) that do not build trust. This shows up in management research: multiple studies show that initial trust both in the individual and in their overall leadership competence is higher for leaders that present as extraverted.[38] We will dive into how quiet leaders can use their strengths and go beyond the stereotypes to build trust on a time scale that allows for getting things done.

---

[38] Joyce Bono and Timothy Judge, "Personality and transformational and transactional leadership: A meta-analysis," *Journal of Applied Psychology* 89 no. 5 (2004): pp. 901–910.

- *Gaining mutual understanding*—Also key to getting things done for your organization through relationships is understanding what's important to each party. This closely flows from trust, which drives an open exchange of ideas that makes mutual understanding possible. Quiet leaders' listening skills and ability to leave space for others come in particularly handy here. More room for others to speak can reveal more data about what drives an individual (especially if you have built trust beforehand). That said, extraverts' ability to match the energy level of their counterpart can build trust sooner. This can allow for more fluid conversations earlier in the relationship about what is most important to each party. We will explore how quiet leaders proceed.
- *Using these components to advance toward share objectives*—Here, quiet leaders will present with a unique style of working with others and we will explore how we move from trust and understanding to mutually beneficial action.

Using the Framework: How Do Quiet Leaders Best Navigate Building Relationships?

Building trust

Quiet leaders are by nature thoughtful, analytical, and listen more then they speak. This can be an asset in building trust in a few ways:

- *Listening*: A quiet leader's ability to listen is exquisitely powerful. Paul, a leader in a software services company, calls his strategy of staying nearly silent in small group meetings and letting the other party do much of the talking "playing dumb." In fact, active listening isn't dumb at all. Saying less and listening more allows the other party to declare their interests and provides Paul with valuable information on what makes them tick. When he does speak, he's more easily able to tailor his message to build rapport. There's a fine balance, of course, between being a quiet listener and giving your counterparts a sense of who you really are (see below).

- *Preparation*: This key component of the Quiet Leader's Toolkit can help greatly with connecting. The ability to prepare and think deeply and analytically about the other party, what drives them, and how to proceed accordingly is an asset, particularly for introverted quiet leaders. Much as with presenting, preparation makes a huge difference for a quiet leader. Before every meeting with a new group or individual, it pays dividends to do some research on a few key "checklist" ideas. These include:

  o   What is my counterpart's background?

  o   What are common connections?

  o   What experiences might color how they view the issues at hand?

  o   What does this mean for information and ideas that may resonate with time?

  Coming prepared helps me focus less on what I want to say and more on the delivery of the message and building authenticity (more on how to do this with larger audiences in the next chapter). Given my quiet nature, budgeting my energy in this arena ensures I make the most out of my interpersonal interactions.

Quiet leaders also tend to process their thoughts internally, usually speak less than others, and are not the loudest people in the room. How can this be a limitation to building trust?

- *Getting others to know you*: Quiet leaders must put in extra effort to counteract the negative assumptions that others may make about them given their reserved nature. Quiet leaders have described this phenomenon to me in a hundred different ways, and I have heard each one from my friends, family, and mentors that I can sometimes seem hard to read and aloof, particularly to extraverts who look for higher baseline level of social reciprocity and emotional feedback in their interactions. This certainly impacts how I communicate with my teammates, and it also has implications as I meet new potential collaborators. For those quiet leaders who are also understated in their emotional reactions, conveying authenticity in your beliefs that you have both verbally and nonverbally can be even more of a struggle, especially if your counterpart is an extravert.

- *Being heard*: For those quiet leaders that are economists with their words, there is sometimes a mismatch between what you think you've said and what you wanted to say. Tim, a scientist who has led hundreds of other scientists at large and small organizations, notes that if he has thought deeply about what is important to say to an individual in a one-on-one interaction, he has a tendency to "under say" it, or say it in a way that's clear to him but may not be fully clear to the listener. To be clear, this is not a one-way street, as oversharing on the details can also leave the listener confused, though many quiet leaders often err on the side of saying too little.

Given their potential limitations, how can quiet leaders grow their ability to build trust with others?

- *Embracing authenticity*: It is often tempting for quiet leaders to "play an extravert" in their interactions with others. I have tried this earlier in my career following well-meaning advice from mentors and friends; I did not get the intended results, and my attempts were often counterproductive. On reflection, I presented in a way not authentic to myself and my counterparts sensed it. Even if your collaborator does not overtly feel you're being disingenuous, inauthenticity can also be insidious. It may result in your counterpart feeling like something's not quite right in their interactions with you. The Quiet Leaders that we've spoken to build authenticity in a variety of ways, reflective of the intention to transparency within the Quiet Leader's Toolkit in Chapter 3:

o *Transparency of information*—There is a school of thought that says that information is power, and holding information increases one's power. For a senior leader (really for anyone), sharing what you know builds great trust and also makes teams run better. Further, quiet leaders who adopt this style can combat the notion that they are "playing their cards close to the vest." Especially for members of my own team, when I prepare for meetings, I will aim to include a section of the discussion where I strive for them to "know what I know." These topics include developments in other departments of relevance to them, interactions I've had with outside collaborators, relevant external developments, and what's on my agenda. Thinking ahead of your interactions on what you can share to expand your transparency can help in this goal. Of course, depending on the topics and your organization, this may not always be possible, but transparency in general is powerful in allowing quiet leaders to build trust beyond their volume or the amplitude of their interactions. Further, it can help the team in general execute better as a side benefit.

o *Transparency of thought*—It's not always common for individuals in their interactions to state explicitly what's on their mind. Doing so can be powerful in enhancing others' sense of your authenticity. Paul, a software executive, uses this as an opportunity to counteract his often-stoic demeanor and less effusive personality. He will note his tendency to under communicate and specifically note he is compensating by being direct. He aims to be vulnerable by noting his quiet demeanor, and being direct helps build trust as it puts into context an affect that, without it, could be seen as aloof and hiding something.

- *Vulnerability*—The vulnerability that Paul uses when he's direct is a powerful strategy to build trust in its own right. Quiet leaders misperceived as aloof, or hard to read, can weave in personal stories that can counteract the misperception their demeanor can create. Tim, a senior executive whose group has grown from two to forty during his company's expansion, identifies strongly as an introvert. He exerts his influence as a leader through a series of one-on-one discussions with key people on his team. As he is more apt to listen than talk and is more of a verbal economist than others, he intentionally mentions something about himself, both something good that happened to him and something that he's struggling with. This has made a difference in the rapport his team has reported feeling with him. Of course, this is a balance. The nature of disclosure that works with your team and what you might do for a prospective investor you have just met will of course vary. In my own experience, quiet leaders typically don't share enough of themselves in most of their interpersonal interactions. It is sometimes useful to go just a little bit out of your comfort zone in vulnerable disclosure to find the right balance. As an example, I often use an anecdote about my kids as a way to find the right balance; first, I enjoy talking about my kids, so it's an authentic way for me to be open and enthusiastic. Further, this is an efficient way to find common ground. I have seen others show great vulnerability and build common ground in multiple other ways, like noting charity work that's inspired by a family member.

- *Consistency*—Mark, a marketing consultant, notes that for long-term relationships, consistency in when you show up and how you show up also builds trust. In his experience, showing up on time, following a reliable interaction cadence with external and internal collaborators, and doing what you say over time can build deep trust independent of your words or affect. Mark sees being on time to meetings as a simple way to show his collaborator that he will do what he says he will do. Further, when follow-ups are required, he aims to knock out the easy ones soon after a meeting to again demonstrate reciprocity and trustworthiness. The actions support trust when, as a quiet leader, sometimes his words and presence don't leap out as immediately.

- *Three dimensional relationships*—Collaboration can also help as you look to build important relationships. What always astounds me is how interconnected we all are, particularly within a given industry or discipline. These connections can be an asset as quiet leaders seek to build trust. As we covered, the reason part of my research on people that I meet focuses on common connections is that this helps break the ice and provides a baseline of trust and understanding that can complement the interaction. As part of preparing for particularly important actions, often our team will seek the advice of a common connection. These connections can offer perspective on the person we will be interacting with and a reference on us. A thoughtful approach to your social media can also help—consistency in who you are and what you and your organization stand for that comes through multiple sources can help as much as a common connection to build trust before you even interact. Indeed, in an increasingly online world, counterparties often do their homework on you as well. Investing in activities such as blog posts and podcasts when appropriate are specific ways you can help others get a deeper sense of who you are even if you aren't the warmest when meeting face to face.

Building Mutual Understanding—How Quiet Leaders Accomplish Their Goals

Space and listening

The strength of quiet leaders in building mutual understanding stems from their ability to listen, analyze, and leave space for others. This can uniquely position quiet leaders to be consensus builders.

The other side of this strength is that if a quiet leader's counterpart is doing all of the talking, there is a risk that the "mutual" part in mutual understanding may not take place. The quiet leaders that we have worked with have used several helpful strategies to ensure that they get their point across even if others are dominating the airtime.

- *The power of restating*—Restating what you thought you heard from your counterparty accomplishes a few important things. First, it sends a strong signal to your counterpart that they were really heard. Even if it turns out you've misunderstood something, most people will be happy to clarify what they meant. That interaction in and of itself can help you build rapport and trust. People are likely to appreciate that you're actively trying to understand them. Restating is a great opportunity to accelerate getting to potential areas of collaboration by creating an opportunity to bridge what you hear with what your goals could be. For example, taking the opportunity to restate a problem your counterpart is facing may give the opportunity to segue into solutions that you can provide. Finally, it is a conversational device helpful to those of us who are miserly with words. Since quiet leaders tend to listen more than they speak, restating is a good opportunity to hold up their end of the conversation.

- *Art of verbal judo*—For quiet leaders who talk a lot less than they listen, sometimes it can be difficult to get your side of the shared objective across. In these situations, I will sometimes use my counterparty's words as a springboard to bring points across. This is not to say one should interrupt the speaker or completely twist the flow of ideas. It does mean that when the speaker mentions something that you agree with, it is an opportunity to agree with it, build on it, and add to it in a way that gets your point across. This is the idea of "yes, and" that originates from improv circles to keep the show building, and it can also keep a two-way conversation building. For example, in a meeting with a key clinician we were looking to partner with, my objective was to educate him about a key scientific aspect of one of our medicines, though he continued to drive the conversation in other directions. Rather than talk over him or subvert the discussion in the first few minutes, I jumped in when he brushed past the topic by saying, "It may be worth amplifying on what you just mentioned," and in so doing, I was able to get my point across without subverting the flow of the conversation.

Taking Mutually Beneficial Action

Sometimes, connecting is simply about building trust and mutual understanding for collaborations that may occur in the future. Other times, there are actions to take to advance your organization. Quiet leaders are as good as anyone in contemplating what might be beneficial to their missions. Moving first to put these potential actions on the table can sometimes be a challenge.

- *Preparation*: Quiet leaders are less likely than their extraverted colleagues to create plans out loud, real time. Often, they will come prepared with ideas for action. If actions come to them in the moment, they tend to be fewer, deeper thoughts, which is an advantage as these deeper thoughts are more likely to be actionable. As part of my preparation for a meeting, I also include my ideal actions to take after an interaction—whether it is a point I hope to get a cross, a next step I'd like a potential recruit or investor to take, or an introduction I'd like to get. This enables me to refer back to this and move efficiently if our mutual understanding supports this.

- *First mover advantages and disadvantages*: That said, the quiet leader is also more likely to contemplate before taking action. More extraverted leaders can often take more ground in finding mutually beneficial actions by virtue of their personality. It would be inauthentic for a quiet leader to try to overpower more extraverted personalities, but there are ways to address the risk that being last to speak reduces your opportunities. First is being prepared with your objectives. Knowing what you'd like to get out of the interaction ahead of time helps you seize on collaborative opportunities quickly an in real time. Second, even if you aren't the first to speak, having your counterpart share even more information about what's important to them can accrue well to building a deeper understanding and refining actions.

- *Action steps*: Taking the initiative at the end of meetings to summarize potential actions can give a quiet leader some opportunity to "grab the ball" that flows naturally from the conversation.

Further, moving first to note potential action steps is a good way to ensure that those actions are the ones you actually want to take. Especially for quiet leaders, it is sometimes awkward to force the action in a meeting to get to this point. Specific phrases can help smoothly transition from discussion to action such as "there are a few ways we can move forward" or "sounds like there are some tangible actions we can take." While a quiet leader may not fill the room with their personality, the energy of moving toward a shared objective goes a long way.

- *Follow through*: There's also an opportunity to couple this with immediate follow through as we discussed in the building trust section of this chapter. Quiet leaders in particular can fill the space that their less outsized personalities leave by very consistently following through what actions that come out of discussions.

Putting It All Together

As the Senator has demonstrated in his daily work, getting the most out of one-on-one connections can make a quiet leader highly effective without being the loudest person in the room. Some intention into building trust by counteracting the misperception of a quiet person as aloof, using the power of restatement and your collaborator's language to advance your agenda, and using the flow of the meeting to drive actions you have prepared for are tested ways to get to tangible collaborative action without having to dominate a conversation. Now that we've explored ways quiet leaders can drive their agendas one-on-one, we'll move on to winning the day when you broadcast your message at a larger scale.

Chapter 7

Building a Following—How to Share Your Vision for Your Organization at a Larger Scale

The art of communicating an organization's priorities on a large scale is the goal of leadership that often gets the most airtime when thinking about how quiet leaders approach the job. It is also a driver of why Boards and managers pass over quiet leaders for positions of responsibility. Management research and experience suggest this tendency is based on the preconceived idea that extraverts are better than quiet leaders at broadcasting a company's mission.[39] On the surface, this seems like a logical conclusion. Leaders do a lot of communicating to their Boards, to their customers, to their employees, the press, and more. It's not surprising many assume extraverts would be far more advantaged in this aspect of leadership than their quieter and introverted colleagues. It turns out that this viewpoint glosses over the many unique strengths

[39] "Analyzing effective leaders: Why Extraverts are not Always the Most Successful Bosses," Knowledge@Wharton (The Wharton School, 2010), https://knowledge.wharton.upenn.edu/article/analyzing-effective-leaders-why-extraverts-are-not-always-the-most-successful-bosses/.

quiet leaders can bring to the table. They can use their unique strengths to their advantage, and find ways to compensate in the few areas where extraverts have more natural aptitude.

Matt's story

Of all people, Matt Johnson is someone you'd least expect to be a quiet leader. Matt runs a business that helps other businesses get noticed whether in traditional ads, social media, or (his specialty) podcasts. Since he founded the business, he tried to build a following for his brand and services aggressively. He went to every networking meeting, signed up for every presentation, interview, and podcast that he could, and built partnerships that required him to support others' business in exchange for visibility. With all of that activity, Matt, a natural introvert, was drained every night and felt like he was getting nowhere. While he had deep conviction on what he was saying and felt he was resonating when he got out there, he hit a wall in terms of how much he could do. He was burned out, unfulfilled, and needed to do something differently.

We will dive into how Matt emerged from his struggle with a style of building a following that worked for him. First, we'll take a step back to break down building a following into its component parts and explore how quiet leaders might approach each one.

Building a Following—What's the Task at Hand?

Like any other activity of leadership, we can break down building a following into the sum of its component parts.

- *Message strategy*
  - o *Creating a distinctive message for your organization*—communicating why your organization exists, why it stands out from the noise, and why people should devote attention, time, and resources to it
  - o *Identifying who might best resonate with the message*—figuring out who needs to know about your organization and why, so that you can invest time accordingly
  - o *Identifying the best venue to reach your target audience*—choosing the right format and medium to achieve your goals. These choices include structured settings such as panels and speeches, and unstructured settings such as conferences and networking events. Some of this strategy speaks to how to meet your potential followers where they are and give your message the best chance to shine. The other strategic aspect of venue selection is as a way for quiet leaders to set the stage to their advantage.
- *Message execution*
  - o In other words, actually delivering the message. All of the best ideas on what will resonate with your desired followers aren't relevant unless you, as the leader and key representative of the mission, can deliver the message with conviction and clarity. There are instances where others in the organization could deliver the message, but other instances where only you as the leader can communicate to get the results you are seeking for your organization.

A Quiet Leader's Advantages and Disadvantages in Building a Following

For quiet leaders, the message strategy component of building your following can often come naturally. Like Matt, quiet leaders are naturally disposed to introspection and access the world through analysis. They are also often comfortable creating content, and are used to thinking very deeply before they speak based on how they are wired. These tendencies can lead themselves to creative messages, and thoughtful ways to identify how best to deliver them.

Where quiet leaders will differ from other leaders the most, and potentially have to overcome some limitations, is message execution. This key aspect of building a following is where we will focus in this section. Indeed, some of the limitations of quiet leaders that we discussed in Chapter 2 become relevant, such as volume bias, speed bias, and (for many quiet leaders) a ceiling on their tolerance for social interaction.

So, What to Do About It?

To get practical about how best to deliver your desired message and get people excited about your cause, we break down the settings in which you can build a following into two key categories:

- Structured engagements (a lecture, or video presentation, or a medium sized group meeting such as an investment pitch)
- Unstructured settings (cocktail parties, conferences)

Let's dive into some of the different settings where you will be called on to share your mission and how you engage them as a quiet leader:

Structured Presentations and Group Meetings

This is where the stereotypical extraverted leader builds the stereotype. Videos of Steve Ballmer's energy-filled presentations to employees and Tony Robbins come to mind. For me, well-meaning professors in business school public speaking courses would play these videos as examples of how to bring life to presentations. These videos made the hurdle of leadership seem higher to me as an introvert. There is not a world where even with the maximum amount of caffeine could get me to the Steve Ballmer level of excitement for anything. As I've learned, there are other ways to go about sharing your vision that feel natural to a quiet leader and the mission and get the job done. Some of the strategies we examined in connecting one-on-one are still useful in groups, as well as some new ones that we will explore.

Preparation is the Base of Engaging Your Audience

The power of preparation within the Quiet Leader's Toolkit is a critical part of engaging effectively. Across all of the effective quiet leaders this book has surveyed, being deeply prepared on your message is the key to getting a point across effectively in a structured setting. This of course means knowing your key points by heart, but it also means understanding the source data behind your points and answers to common questions that may come up. Jennifer Kahnweiler's review of influencing tactics for introverts notes two important reasons why message preparation is so critical to broadcasting your message. First, being prepared creates space for creative thought on what will resonate with the listener. Further, it provides a regenerative venue for quiet leaders through the reflection required to prepare.[40]

---

[40]   Jennifer B. Kahnweiler, *Quiet Influence: The introvert's guide to making a difference* (San Francisco, CA: Berrett-Koehler Publishers, 2013).

The other important benefit of getting your message ingrained in your memory is that it enables focus on those elements that come less naturally for quiet leaders. That "muscle memory" for the message enables a quiet leader to devote more energy to the actual delivery of ideas. This includes overcoming volume bias and a less animated effect to leave your listeners feeling your conviction around your message. For example, a prepared quiet leader has more mental bandwidth to focus on emphasis through verbal methods like vocal inflection and nonverbal methods like moving about the stage to connect with different parts of the audience and making appropriate use of hand gestures. All of this said, it bears noting that only that level of animation that feels authentic is the right level. Mike Gilman, a quiet leader and serial entrepreneur in the life sciences industry, finds the balance between preparation and spontaneity by memorizing the first few sentences of his remarks. This way, he has a natural "starter" to help him get over initial nerves. By not memorizing the rest of the talk, he keeps his delivery spontaneous and original, which helps especially when he needs to give the same version of a talk to multiple audiences.

Using Your Strengths as a Quiet Leader to Build Authentic Connection With a Group

While delivery is important, quiet leaders can invest their mental energy during an engagement in something even more important: building a deep connection with their audience. Being the loudest, most dazzling person in the room is far less important than making a connection with the audience. A quiet leader's measure of success in a structured engagement with potential followers is the degree of connection with an audience, not how animated he or she is in their presentation. This concept merits a deeper examination.

Tim Herbert, a self-described quiet leader that has made a career as a tech entrepreneur, has contended with severe dyslexia that impacts his ability to remember and pronounce common words. His fear of making these errors made public speaking difficult and he often presents as a quiet speaker. Through years of practice (and a crash course as an instructor in the military) he has found his style. Much of his overcoming these hurdles have been shifting his measure of success. His success comes when he feels he's made a connection with at least one audience member. He uses strategies to engage the audience that reinforce that feedback he gets that keeps him going through the engagement. I've had the pleasure of speaking to folks that have been in the audience when Tim is speaking. He always gets buy-in for his points through the stories he tells. Even when he is saying something controversial, his listeners have become emotionally invested enough in the very authentic, very vulnerable stories Tim tells that they want to agree with him in spite of themselves.

Let's dive into some of the strategies Tim and others use to dial up the passion and conviction that your listeners need to see to begin to feel that same passion.

- **Storytelling**—Tim Herbert found that when he encapsulated his key points in the form of stories, it became easier to overcome his fear of speaking. He found he could convey his points with more conviction, commit them to "muscle memory," and focus his time on how best to connect with the audience. Why did his listeners think his stories were so effective? His listeners note that he goes beyond the "fake vulnerability" many speakers attempt. In these instances, a speaker might note a personal failing but do so with generic language that glosses over the struggle that went with the setback. In contrast, Tim's listeners note that his stories are vulnerable, raw, and sometimes even a little uncomfortable. This feeling makes them want to root for Tim and primes them to work with Tim to buy into what he's trying to convey. Consider a few key points when you choose your own stories to connect:

o   *The stories that are most powerful draw from your authentic experience*: Here, the intention to transparency in the Quiet Leader's Toolkit is helpful. Quiet leaders sometimes struggle with appearing human and vulnerable, and stories that show some of this side of you can be highly effective. This could be a professional challenge and how you overcame it, or how a particular incident (a patient with disease, for example) made you feel, or some details of your personal journey that got you to your current position. It may feel awkward or inconsistent with your career goals to risk showing some vulnerability. Bouncing ideas off of a trusted friend or mentor can help you find stories in your personal experience that are both authentic and appropriate to what you'd like your audience to know about you.

o   *Find the balance on depth*: Stories should be deep enough to feel real, but not so detailed that you lose your listeners. In this era of smartphones and conflicting priorities, the time you have to "set the hook" is short. For an opening story, two to three minutes is plenty so you can get to the meat of the presentation.

o   *Create a point of reference during your remarks*: In the improv world, this is called "reincorporation" or bringing back an idea from a previous scene. If you have chosen your story well, referring back to it during or at the close of your remarks can rekindle some of the positive emotions you were able to convey with a story.

- **Feel the message**—In my own experience, a message that I have deeply thought through and believe in flows naturally to a presentation that connects with my audience. I've felt a noticeable difference in the passion with which I communicate after I have thought through all of the points and counterpoints of the arguments I'm making to join our cause. At that point, I am no longer performing but instead communicating strong points for which I have built deep conviction. For example, when I am pitching the unique aspects of one of the medicines our companies have developed, I often think through both why the message makes sense and also common objections that I think my listeners should have before they are convinced of my point. When I know we have cogent answers to these questions, it helps quiet my internal monologue about whether the message is resonating. This in turn allows me to focus more on connecting with my audience.

- **Own your limitations**—Some of the strategies that work when connecting one-on-one can also work with an audience, such as making yourself vulnerable specifically by noting your quiet nature. Matt Johnson notes that admitting he is a quiet leader up front in a presentation energizes him and gives him a head start in connecting with his audience. For Matt, it gives him permission not to be something other than his authentic self and also creates a small degree of vulnerability that helps him build trust with his audience. I have used this to great effect as well—noting my quiet demeanor for points that the listener should be particularly excited about. In other words, if a quiet leader like me is excited by that point, it is truly exciting.

- **Preparation specifically for connection**—A particularly useful exercise prior to a presentation is going deep on the audience—their background, their interests, their potential biases and what matters to them. If you are speaking at a gathering, getting a list of attendees or at least a sense of common characteristics of the attendees is a good way to prepare. As much as it can drain me, if I have an opportunity the day before or even a few hours before to circulate around, I can be part of interactions at a conference that give me a flavor of the audience—for example, the kinds of questions they ask at other sessions. That level of familiarity focuses me on the task of addressing their needs which also helps me stay present. Further, what I learn gives me material that I can reference to find connection and commonality with the audience. For example, referring to a common experience such as an evening event or referencing an audience member that had been a speaker previously are ways to build a bridge to your listeners.

- **Listen closely—trial and error**—The best way to figure out whether something works for you is to try it. Did a turn of phrase or a point in time in which you amplified volume or made an emphasis resonate with the audience? Did more heads nod? In subsequent conversations did that phrase stick with folks? Importantly—how did that feel for you? Did it feel forced or natural after a few tries? Again, preparation matters—sometimes there's no better preparation than going out and making your pitch and tweaking on the fly. Especially for quiet leaders, if you have the ability to arrange your structured presentations so that your most important ones are later in your sequence of presentations, this will accrue to your benefit. Everyone needs a warmup, but quiet leaders who need to devote more of their intention to presenting a message benefit from warmups and practice even more than most.

Unstructured Settings

Structured settings, while draining for quiet leaders sometimes, allow for quiet leaders to prepare since most times, the subject of the meeting and agenda items are communicated in advance of the discussion. Unstructured settings can be even more daunting; these are the cocktail parties and conferences that also stereotypically are not the realm of quiet leaders. For me, these events take a lot of "activation energy" (as my chemistry colleagues call it), or energy just to show up and be effective. Especially for introverted quiet leaders, these events are overstimulating and draining both because of the volume of interpersonal contact but also because quiet leaders can feel (I certainly do) that they are not doing all they can for their organizations by gutting out these events despite their best efforts. While this is not always true, unstructured settings are one of the few places that serendipity can happen and as such are critical to accomplishing your objectives. So how do we get through them and maximize our effectiveness?

- **Make a plan**—Success at unstructured events is not about quantity, it's about quality. Again, preparation can help quiet leaders. Often these events have invitee lists or lists of panels. Investing some time ahead of the meeting to highlight those people, panels, or interactions that would be most impactful help narrow the field. Further, if attendee lists are not available, mindfulness about the types of interactions most impactful to your organization at this conference can help. You can focus your energies and intention on those goals; this of course does not mean willfully ignoring other well-meaning eventgoers, but it does mean you might be easier on yourself when not making a priority interaction, or giving yourself permission to gracefully exit once your "to-do" list is all complete.

- **Focus on connection**—It is human nature to retreat into your shell when you see your extraverted colleagues getting the lion's share of attention. You may feel they are accomplishing their objectives with seeming ease and making you look less like a captain of industry in the process in your own perception. However, much as Tim Herbert learned to do in his public speaking, focusing on connection over feeling like you're the most interesting person in the room will yield dividends. Sure, the extraverts in your small cocktail party conversation might be the life of the party; however, there are ways to build connection as a quiet leader (especially for those individuals you prioritized). A few questions to ask yourself as you make the rounds at an unstructured event. For the individuals on your priority list:
  - o Did you use your listening skills to make the individuals on your priority list feel like you genuinely cared about what they had to say?
  - o Learn something new about them?
  - o Find something that you can follow-up about?
- **Quiet leaders have different ways to get to "yes" on this checklist**—and doing your homework on a priority connection can help. If you have read ahead of time about his/her background, you can think of a few questions to ask them that can convey your genuine interest in them (see also the connecting chapter for some advice on how to prepare to have an optimal connection). Often, though, individuals you meet are ones you didn't get a chance to learn about beforehand. Here, quiet leaders can still prepare with a few key points they want to convey about themselves and questions they'd like to ask someone they

meet. Personally, I'm not a fan of the gimmicky oddball questions some of the networking books suggest. In my experience, the key is choosing a way to convey interest in your counterpart that is authentic to you.

- **Set the rules of the game**—As a quiet leader, you can set the field to your advantage to maximize the gain and minimize how much it exhausts you. Are there choices to be had? Choose small group dinners over raucous bar events; choose the less-crowded room or table. If you are entering a cocktail discussion, choose the groups that are smallest and quietest, or better yet, find the folks that may be also looking for someone to chat with. This way, you have a chance to use your strong listening skills and not fight for airtime with the louder folks in the room. Chip Clark, a CEO of a biotechnology company, actually books connecting flights through obscure airports during his industry's annual conference in San Francisco when he travels from Boston. This way, he can avoid draining social interaction when most of the industry takes the same flights over to the conference, and he can be on top of his game at high priority events.

- **Focus on follow-up**—especially for those folks that you have prioritized, follow-up is key for quiet leaders. You can use a thoughtfully worded social media connection or email to emphasize what was important and build the bridge for the future. Further, as was true in a one-to-one setting, following up as promised after a group networking event builds trust more than a dazzling conversation.

Beyond the Podium or Cocktail Party— "Systems" Strategies

Beyond what you do as an individual to share your message (or "wave the flag" as we call it at our companies), taking advantage of the resources you have and the team you've built to amplify your message can be effective as well. Here, the power of collaboration and systematic thinking from the Quiet Leader's Toolkit come into play. As your organization scales its resources, building a system of communication that goes well beyond what you do as an individual allows a quiet leader to transcend being a "hero" to share an organization's mission and spread the mission in a systematized, distributed, and ultimately effective way.

Make Building a Following a Team Sport

Like any other key strategic function, good leaders complement themselves and delegate where possible to folks with those complementary skills. Effective communication of the mission is no different. The extraverts on our team are often natural presenters, give us some energy to play off of when we are discussing our organization's mission, and allow us to expand the breadth of who knows us when a quiet leader's natural tendency is to be narrower and deeper. It should be noted that there is no substitute for senior leaders, quiet or not, for being out front with the message. However, finding the right extraverts to complement you ensures that you're not draining yourself on every last discussion and have a chance to raise the level of energy in the room. Further, the contrast between a quiet leader's style and an extraverts can highlight your message when you do speak.

Teams that know each other well can also play off of each other to maximize an interaction. For example, my teammates will sometimes make good-natured jokes at my expense when we are on the road with investors we know well. For example, they'll refer to me tongue-in-cheek as "the boss" and highlight my unique choice of words in certain situations (such as the word *effectuate*, which the team loves). They do this with purpose, as the jokes lighten the mood and give me an opportunity to break my often very serious, intense demeanor as well as showcase the authentic team dynamic we have.

Use Social Media to Clear the Runway

So now back to Matt, who was naturally prone to introspection as an introvert—and he realized that in his zeal to evangelize his mission to the fullest, he was both not being thoughtful on where he was focused. He found better mediums for his message that suited his style. He winnowed down his networking and partnering engagements, focusing only on those most likely to advance the business. Ultimately, he settled on podcasts since they amplified his message, allowed him to be thoughtful about what he presented, and could be used and shared widely. This worked so well for him that he ended up focusing his business on the podcasts and how other businesses might raise their profile through this medium.

In today's age, capturing a great message and amplifying it via social media can be a great way to take the pressure off of networking events. Mike Gilman has used Twitter to build connections with a variety of individuals in his industry that he otherwise would not have met. When he does get to in-person events at industry conferences, he has a head start in that he knows some proportion of the attendees through social media (or they know him). Well-thought-out podcasts, blog posts, and social media presence can give people a sense of who you are even before you walk in the room. Social media can complement a quiet leader's natural tendency to be narrower and deeper in the way they evangelize an organization's mission. Further, it's efficient. If done well, good blog posts can pay dividends for years. Again, here, intention matters as poorly done social media can pay the kind of dividends you don't want for years as well. Finally, it bears emphasizing that in many cases, there is no substitute for your own voice and (live) presence in sharing the mission.

Further, like networking in unstructured events, a "spray and pray" approach to social media is less effective than a targeted one. As always, it pays to be thoughtful about who you want to reach, how they are best reached, what threads you want to highlight. Further, as a quiet leader, it's worth reflecting on some important questions to figure out which venue is right for you.

- Do you prefer the spoken or written word?
- Which one reaches the broadest audience in your field?
- Which one allows you to most sustainably project your passion for your mission?
- Which medium can you commit to a sustained presence?

For me, the written word through blog posts and social media has been my answer as I can expend comparatively less energy writing than I can summoning my best self for a podcast or video. Quiet leaders who can summon a lively, engaging presence in curated bursts may lean toward the short video format where you can make a few key points about your mission and upload them on social media or your organizational website. Others may like the conversational format of being a voice on social media. This still allows a quiet leader to titrate their energy and be a presence on their terms without having to be the loudest person in the room.

Find Your Release Valve to Build Your Reserves

This chapter aims to find ways to authentically and systematically spread your mission around the world without having to go beyond a comfortable level of social interactions. That all said, inevitably there will be times when your mission requires you to be in front of more humans than you'd like to be as a quiet leader. You might be in the middle of an organization altering period of time, such as a fundraising campaign or a product rollout. Further, you might be draining your human interaction reserves outside of the office, such as attending a family wedding. Quiet leaders who make time for "release valves" find themselves more ready to take on these unplanned gauntlets. Further, they are more likely to be effective when they commit to the calendar to network. These activities might include exercise, a solitary hobby, or writing. During a particularly grueling period of fundraising, I found great stability learning carpentry. My wife can attest to the periods of time that are socially intense on the job as somehow that's the time the wood paneled walls and bookshelves seem to multiply at our house. Even though these periods can be busy, making time for these releases is all the more crucial such that each interaction becomes an opportunity and not a chore.

Wherever Possible Commit Building a Following to Routine

Building a following for quiet leaders can be a lift, and a necessary one. All of the strategies we have noted—preparation, focusing on connection, preserving authenticity, listening well, using your team, and controlling the field of play—can help make this exercise feel authentic, create effective connections, and ultimately potentially be an energizing part of leading. The final part of the strategy is thinking systematically and committing to sharing your message in a stepwise, structured process. It is somewhat like moving your running shoes to near your bed in the morning increases the likelihood you actually take that morning run.

For leaders who are solo or part of lean teams, setting a time each week where you focus on social media, or commit to doing a presentation or networking event can help you make it happen. For larger organizations, delegating to someone to make sure they are systematizing getting you and your team "out there" helps counteract a quiet leader's natural tendency to avoid some of these interactions. Finally, realizing that quiet leaders have strengths in other areas, be kind to yourself. You may not be able to network into the late hours of the night like your extraverted colleagues, and it may take more work to connect with an audience when you are at the podium. But, as we have gone into in prior chapters, you as a quiet leader have strengths others don't and can use the tools we've discussed to nonetheless find a way to make your message resonate with your audience.

Chapter 8

Collaborating in an Extraverted World

As a female physician in an extravert and male-dominated academic department, Lalitha felt that she was always fighting uphill. A quiet leader by nature, she was naturally great at listening to her patients and finding creative ways to think about clinical trials that find answers for some very scary diseases. Where she felt she struggled was when it came time to present work collaboratively with her peers. In group meetings, she felt overshadowed by her extraverted colleagues, and often felt she had lost something in these interactions. She felt that those that spoke the loudest most often walked out of those discussions with more, whether it was credit for collaborative work or new opportunities. She wanted to find an authentic way to engage with this team assertively, as she felt she was not currently doing right by her career or ultimately her patients.

Lalitha's experience is unfortunately not unique for quiet members of teams. Quiet leaders don't lead in a vacuum. They need to coexist as peers and collaborators with extraverts, in a business world (especially in the U.S.) that values extraversion. Further, in our current post-pandemic world, there are unique considerations for how quiet leaders inhabit the team environment. We will dive into how you use the tools at your disposal to collaborate in a world of extraverts. For extraverts, we will also provide some practical suggestions on how to best work with the quiet colleagues around you.

Addressing Common Areas of Friction Between Quiet Leaders and Extraverts on a Team

Many of the strategies within the Quiet Leader's Toolkit can be helpful when collaborating with your peers. However, there are special considerations we'll focus on that are most relevant when you're not "in charge" of those with whom you work. We will focus on how quiet leaders can pragmatically navigate these potential friction points.

Airtime and sharing credit

Intuitively, as it did in Lalitha's case, it stands to reason that quiet leaders risk receiving less airtime than their extraverted colleagues. Airtime can mean multiple things in a collaborative context; it can mean the amount a collaborator speaks in group meetings and how influential those words are with decisionmakers present. In a related phenomenon, quiet leaders also risk receiving less credit when there is credit to be shared.

You may be part of a leadership team vying for the boss's attention, part of a working group of fellow leaders trying to craft a consensus guideline, or part of a delegation of leaders trying to communicate their agenda to policymakers. Going "head-to-head" and trying to talk over the extraverts will feel inauthentic and likely be ineffective. Further, trying to wrest the credit from the loudest person in a group may also feel unnatural. Still, it's professionally necessary to ensure that you and your organization get the visibility you need. So how best to for quiet leaders to stand their ground amongst a group of extraverts?

- **Use the process to your advantage**: For those instances where you have to match airtime with extraverted colleagues in a peer setting, using the structure of the meeting or engagement can help you. For example, having an agenda for meetings ahead of time can focus the discussion and enable quiet leaders to prepare for the give and take that extraverts enjoy and use to make progress. If nobody is setting the agenda, taking the opportunity to do so can allow you to drive the conversation without needing to fight through the noise during the discussion. In a panel discussion setting, setting up or requesting a prep call to focus the discussion, or submitting topics to the moderator beforehand can use process to enable you to get your points across.

- **Verbal judo**: Many quiet leaders have commented that the way to cut into a conversation dominated by extraverts is to build off of what's being said. This is more graceful and natural for many quiet leaders looking to jump into the exchange than trying to dominate from the outset. I often try to reference the comments of others earlier in the dialogue and use that as a springboard to make a comment (prior preparation helps for quiet leaders to have such comments top of mind); for example, you might say "To build off of the point [extravert] made earlier…" or "I'm glad [extravert] brought this up, as I've been thinking…" Statements such as these also have the side benefit of building a relationship with your fellow collaborators as you've now noted that you've listened and valued what they've said.

- **Quality and Mission over Quantity**: One of the hardest things for me as an introvert are the group panel discussions including my CEO peers, where other constituents like investors, future employees may be there and will be "judging" you. I often see dynamics where CEOs feel the pressure and feel compelled to speak for the sake of doing so, or they will one up each other in promoting themselves. For a quiet leader, this feels inauthentic and often a bit silly. In many ways, it is. Give yourself the permission to ask the one question that best advances your mission, and avoid asking questions simply to "be heard" as the downside is that those questions may be less mission-centric.

- **Benefit of allies**: The power of collaboration from the Quiet Leader's Toolkit can also help. Lalitha has noted, she has sometimes employed an extraverted counterpart to help amplify her message. She will sometimes preview ideas with members of the group. With the benefit of understanding why it's good for the organization and for them, they can lend their voice particularly in larger group meetings where sometimes her voice alone may not be enough. Preparation can be helpful in setting the stage for using allies—being clear and convinced yourself about your message can facilitate seeking out the appropriate allies and bringing them around to your point of view. Building strong enough relationships to seek allies in the group setting requires some intention to connect on a one-to-one basis with your colleagues (see Chapter 6 for more on how best to do this).

- **The power of "I"**: Karl Moore, an Associate Professor of Management at McGill University, writes that quiet leaders, particularly those earlier in their careers, shouldn't be afraid to use the word "I" sometimes in their group work to claim those portions of the work that they own.[41] We are acculturated since

---

[41] Karl Moore, "How to Stand Out at Your First Job, the Introvert Way," Quiet Revolution, https://www.quietrev.com/how-to-stand-out-at-your-first-job-the-introvert-way/.

elementary school to acknowledge our teams and use "we." For quiet leaders, however, some tactful commentary in a way that feels authentic to you can establish what you bring to the table. For example, noting your role on the team if you are introducing yourself to the group for the first time, or being the one to present group work can be a tactful way to ensure you are recognized for your efforts rather than lost in the group. Further, if you are going to stake your claim to your work, noting the parts that required collaborators can help find the I/we balance that's expected of quiet leaders even if the extraverts are getting more credit.

- **Be open**: Earlier in my career, I would go into collaborations on the defensive, assuming that the extraverts in the room were out to take credit for my hard-earned work. For an introvert like me, the combination of my quiet nature and my initial mistrust did not help me collaborate with my peers even when my goals depended on it. It is important to remember that extraverts talk to think, where quiet leaders think before they talk. Some of the airtime balance is simply extraverts getting their mental wheels turning. Further, the key needs of extraverts are correlated with collaboration, given extraverts' desire to have a sounding board and work in an environment with more external stimulation. Starting out with an open mindset ensures you have a chance to be at your best (and adjust if necessary) when you choose to collaborate.

To build on the lessons of Chapter 5, if you are the leader of a team or the organizer of an event that includes quiet leaders and extraverts, a few steps can support a healthy dynamic. This is important, as a team of collaborators that feel that credit is distributed according to volume and not merit will not perform with the interests of your mission as their primary focus. Meeting structure is one way to level the playing field for quiet leaders. Leaders and event organizers can distribute airtime through the structure of a panel process by using an agenda, pre-agreed topics, and pre-agreed sequence of speakers. Ben Dattner, author of the *Blame Game*, suggests amending the format of engaging at meetings to elicit feedback from quiet leaders, especially at larger meetings; additions to the format could include breakout groups, polls, or chat functions using Zoom or other available technologies.[42]

How you show up as a quiet leader can also level the playing field, when you take intention to see the contributions of all members of a team effort, and model this by deflecting credit that you might take yourself toward others. Though everyone has an ego to some degree, quiet leaders often authentically embrace the value of humility as they're not the first to speak. In an image-obsessed world where social media incentivizes us to glorify ourselves, I've found that people are attracted to a humble leaders and that companies that foster this dynamic are an attractive place for new employees to join. Further, by exhibiting this behavior, you are sending a message that jockeying for credit is not a valued activity at your organization. This allows quiet leaders and extraverts to focus on doing their best work for the mission.

Generating ideas

Extraverts and quiet leaders, by nature, create ideas and put them into motion in different ways. We touched on some of these phenomena in Chapter 5 in the context of team leadership. Different strategies may make sense when interacting with ones' peers and colleagues. Extraverts tend to think out loud and see collaboration as an iterative process where ideas are "hashed out" through wide ranging discussion. This may be exhausting for you as a quiet leader, where you may prefer to think in

---

[42] Susan Cain, "How to Level the Playing Field for Introverts and Extroverts," https://www.quietrev.com/level-playing-field-introverts-extroverts/.

solitude and come with more fully baked ideas. Relative to leading a team, working with a peer may afford you fewer options to set the field of play in a way best suited to you. However, there is value in being upfront about how you create ideas, and meeting your extraverted colleagues partway. A few ways to do this include scheduling a session to brainstorm rather than allowing for a number of impromptu sessions, and setting up a timeline for a project that allows you to go away and think of ideas you can bring to the table and iterate with your colleagues. Gustavo Rizzetti, who runs a coaching consultancy, suggests an exercise that may be helpful for mixed extravert/quiet leader teams to do where, before beginning a project, participants plot themselves on two axes: outgoing versus shy, and whether they "talk to think" or "think to talk." This way all parties know where each other stand and can account for this as the project gets underway.[43]

Making decisions

Often (but not always) correlated with quiet leadership is the speed at which an individual is ready to make a decision. When collaborating with extraverts, it is important to set some ground rules up front about how to get to a decision. Here, the lessons from Chapter 5 about assessing and quantifying conviction will be important to apply in the peer setting. Some members of a group (who often tend to be quiet leaders) may want to consider and incorporate the merits of a particular decision before they're bought in, and others may have strong opinions but as quiet leaders may not express them as strongly as they feel about the issue. Further, the idea of leaving space (such as a twenty-four-hour rule) for the group to come to a true consensus also apply. On the other pole,

---

[43] Gustavo Razzetti, "About Fearless Culture: Culture Change Consultancy," Fearless Culture, https://www.fearlessculture.design/about.

it is important to set definitive timelines for decisions, as the extraverts and faster deciders in the room will become frustrated and impatient once they feel the group has reached the right answer. An important difference in this situation relative to the one in Chapter 5 is that peer groups may not have an obvious hierarchical leader. Team members can help facilitate full representation of ideas by speaking up when we feel the group hasn't considered all view points, or is moving faster (or slower) than pre-agreed ground rules suggest. Leaders who might ultimately oversee peer group interactions can facilitate this balance by supporting and if necessary, enforcing the ground rules that a group of peers sets ahead of time. While extraverts may want to get cracking once they feel they have a handle on the issues, we as quiet leaders will need to hold the line and respect the processes set out by the team.

Mentoring Quiet Leaders

Part of the joy of building your leadership skills is the opportunity to share these skills with others. If you choose to be a mentor, tailoring your approach when you are mentoring a quiet leader makes a big difference. Extravert and quiet leaders may have different ways of demonstrating their readiness for the next level. Further, they will have different challenges to overcome when they ascend to leadership. The most important thing you can do for a quiet leader is to help them embrace how to advance their career and still be authentic to themselves. There are a few important ways quiet leaders have noted where mentors can help the most:

- **Navigate process to their advantage**: Coming up as an employee, the most useful advice mentors have given me is how to navigate an organization's culture and processes to my advantage. For example, a quiet leader mentee might benefit from your view on how to shine out in an organization in ways that don't require fighting with extraverts for airtime. This might include advice on what events are likely to be most valuable as they prioritize their engagement in these energy-draining affairs. It may also include ways quiet leaders can use the processes within the company to demonstrate their leadership (such as taking charge of a key committee or company event) in ways other than trying to outshine their louder counterparts.

- **Guide on when it matters to push themselves**: Also, as a mentor, you'll have the experience to know when to motivate your mentees to push themselves outside of their comfort zone. For example, it can help when a mentor pushes their mentee to attend that critical cocktail party where key decision makers might be present. Specific advice on how to fulfill their goals works better than general statements (just get out there, smile more, be livelier, and so forth) that don't embrace the selectivity quiet leaders need to exhibit to stay authentic to themselves.

- **Modulate their self-critic**: Emerging quiet leaders are acutely aware of working in an extraverted world. Introspective by nature, it is easy for them to ruminate on whether they were effective in leadership settings, particularly when extraverts seemed to dominate the proceedings. As a mentor, you can provide some important perspective—sometimes (often!) quiet leaders are more effective even when fighting for airtime with extraverts than they think they are. Perspective can also mean constructive feedback and focused suggestions when the limitations of quiet leadership do show up in a mentee's career progression. For example, hearing from a trusted mentor about how others may perceive you as cold or aloof given your quiet nature is a good, safe starting place to take stock of how you might use the Quiet Leader's Toolkit to take a different approach.

Navigating the Post-Pandemic Hybrid World as a Quiet Leader

The events beginning in March 2020 and the explosion of remote working have been a sea change for how we lead. For quiet leaders, it has created an entirely different way of accessing leadership. Some of the draining parts of collaborating in the office environment (large meetings, office cocktail parties) have simply not been feasible in the setting of the pandemic. Further, the opportunity to be more selective about group interactions has given quiet leaders a greater opportunity to recharge. This is now changing in many venues to a hybrid environment, and, although it's unclear where our working norms will eventually land as the pandemic evolves, it seems clear how we work won't be the same again. For quiet leaders in particular, there are many opportunities and a few challenges to consider in navigating the "new normal":

- **Hybrid work offers a new degree of prioritization for you as a leader**: The widespread availability of video conferencing and the acceptability of using it even for high stakes interactions create opportunities to bring your best self to each interaction. Chip Clark, the biotech CEO we met in Chapter 6, notes that he has been better able to manage the limitations of being a quiet leader now that even the highest stakes interactions such as Board meetings and multimillion dollar deal negotiations in his industry can take place via video conference. There are many more opportunities to recharge and get into your comfort zone when working from home without compromising business objectives. He has noticed that he can take on many more opportunities to connect and broadcast his mission with this new flexibility.

There are also many new opportunities to be selective that being in the office didn't afford. Especially for quiet leaders running their teams, and for the quiet leaders on your team, aiming to return to a 100 percent "face-time" culture may miss some opportunities to get the most out of your and others' leadership. For example, not every meeting requires quiet leaders' in-person presence—if someone else is running the meeting, for instance, and you are there to listen, you may be able to participate remotely and reserve your energy elsewhere. However, if you are presenting, part of a celebration, rallying the troops, or navigating a potentially contentious topic, being in person makes a huge difference. Some degree of intention helps here: our team has left the middle days of the week for collaborative meetings while aiming for individual and more tactical work at the tail ends of the week. This way, the quiet leaders on our team can recharge but bring their energy to collaboration when it's time.

- **Resist the temptation to crawl completely into your shell**: This all said, just because you now have a (very plausible) reason to engage in leadership from the solitary comfort of your home office, it is important to have some perspective. David, a quiet leader by nature who leads a twenty-person group at his startup, noticed himself starting to pull back from the types of opportunities to connect that in the past he might have attended. Under the guise of being more productive, it became very easy to participate in everything via video screen. Even as vaccination gave him the opportunity to engage his colleagues in person, he found himself driven by the inertia of continuing to use the video conference or not participating at all. In contrast, prior to the pandemic, he would use some of the strategies we discussed in Chapter 6 to engage when it was consistent with his mission. Now, he had gotten into the habit of avoiding these opportunities. Public health considerations are paramount, though as quiet leaders it's important to ensure we stay in the habit of connecting when it's relevant to our missions. Even though many tasks can be done now virtually, there are still some, such as refreshing relationships with your colleagues, that can't be replicated over Zoom.

- **Pay special attention to the extraverts and their transition to hybrid work**: Aoife, the biotech executive, notes that the hybrid work of the pandemic has hit extraverts on her team particularly hard. Extraverts need interaction to gain energy, drive their thought processes and get things done. Specific strategies are important to recreate this energy and get the greatest contribution from your team's extraverts even in the new normal.

  o *Recreating the "drop in"*—Much as we learned in Chapter 5 the value of impromptu conversations for engaging extraverts, virtual platforms like Zoom, Teams, or even the good old fashioned cell phone can help recreate this. I try to call extraverts on my team "out of the blue" rather than email when I'm wondering about something complex—it's not a substitute for the office brainstorm, but it certainly helps increase the energy quotient for extraverts. If time is short to call all of the extraverts on your team, even the unscheduled text or chat function if your organization has it can help extraverts feel the spontaneous interaction that they're missing from the in-person setting.

  o *Prioritizing collaboration time*—Quiet leaders on your team can benefit from fixed times for team collaboration as they can prepare for it and schedule regenerative solitary work outside of these hours. Extraverts can also benefit because putting collaboration on the schedule means it will happen and happen regularly. In the setting of the pandemic, making time (even if it's not how you think as a quiet leader) to brainstorm ideas with extraverts can help them stay engaged. Having a predictable cadence of collaborative discussion maximizes the chance that more collaborators will be in the same physical space at the same time. This can also facilitate the impromptu interactions that bring the best out of extraverts.

o *Structured community*—Another missing element from office culture during the era of remote work has been the informal sense of "water cooler" community that one gets from regular interaction at the office. In an era where many workers choose to engage remotely and heterogeneously when they do collaborate, some structure and intention helps to create community. At the companies I have led, we have assigned all new employees mentors with basic expectations on how they interact and how often. We've used technology to create random conversations that team members can choose to opt into or not, to create an opportunity for the types of impromptu conversations that build connection, create idea exchange, and also regenerate the extraverts on our team. Finally, each team has an expectation to get together at least virtually on a periodic basis. The virtual format creates space for the quiet leaders on teams, and the fact that we are having opportunities to interact is important to the extraverts.

Overall, the companies I've led have benefited from an emphasis on flexibility as we've navigated the pandemic. These events layer complexity on what is already a complex endeavor of leading a diverse group of people engaging in a complex undertaking. What works for some parts of the organization may not work for others, and leaving space for team members to find what works for them preserves their energy for the mission rather than trying to conform their personality or habits to a rigid ideal. Practically, this means flexibility in *how* people work as long as they deliver, and flexibility in how you as a leader communicate with different parts of the organization. While the degree of flexibility available will depend on the nature of work (for example, surgeons can't work from home), an effort toward flexibility can allow your quiet leaders in particular to do their best work.

We've walked through the unique opportunities and challenges that quiet leaders have, provided a framework to understand if you are a quiet leader, and now have walked through some of the key activities of leading. Many of these strategies are designed to help quiet leaders contend with their status as outside of the norm for leadership. There is a special cohort of quiet leaders that are outside of the mainstream not only through personality, but also because of their race, gender, or other key characteristics. I detail their unique experiences in the next chapter, and how to use the Quiet Leader's toolkit in these circumstances.

Chapter 9

Quiet Leadership in a Diverse World

The strategies within this book are relevant to all quiet leaders, regardless of your industry, age, gender, and nationality. However, personality type is only one facet of a person. Leaders bring all of our background and experiences to leadership. Further, we live in a world that increasingly seeks to expand the diversity of our leadership ranks to look more like those we lead. As such, increasingly often, a quiet leader's diversity of personality intersects with other elements of the diversity framework. Diversity brings many unique strengths to quiet leaders. As it relates to quiet leadership, being from outside of the mainstream background also brings unique hurdles to overcome. This chapter dives into the intersection of quiet leadership and other elements of diversity. It provides specific advice for quiet leaders who also bring other aspects of themselves to leadership, whether across gender, culture, or otherwise, that are not "typical" for a leader. Further, for those quiet leaders from the mainstream, it can provide some context for how you can lead a diverse team and make space for your fellow quiet leaders' experience.

The "Double Outsider" phenomenon: The quiet leader's version

Many of the quiet leaders who come from different backgrounds spoke to the phenomenon of being a "double outsider." That is, they felt the combination of their quiet personalities and their age, race, culture, physical characteristics, gender, or orientation put them doubly outside of the dominant (extraverted, white, athletic, and male) leadership ideal either in their organizations or in society at large. On top of not being extraverts, they did not look like, sound like, or come from the same parts of the world as the leaders currently in charge and those making their way through the ranks. The term "double outsider" has been in currency for many years; we use the term as it relates to the intersection of quiet leadership and other traits that are outside of the mainstream for the ideal leaders.[44] Both for those aspiring to leadership and those already leading, these quiet leaders felt that being a double outsider posed unique challenges. The phenomenon is widespread enough that it has even inspired movements and groups dedicated to it. For example, Jeri Bingham, a self-proclaimed introvert and organizational behavior doctoral student, instituted "Black Introvert Week" during Black History Month to raise awareness for and further explore the intersection between introversion and race.[45] Instagram's #blackintrovert is another medium exploring this intersection. Simon Bridges, a former leader of New Zealand's government, is a self-described introvert and grew up

---

[44] Jessica Faye Carter, *Double Outsiders: How Women of Color can Succeed in Corporate America* (Minneapolis, MN: Jist Works, 2007).

[45] Darcel Rockett, "Black Introvert Week Is a Time for Quiet Folks to Toot Their Horns, Thanks to Jeri Bingham, Who Created the 'Hush Loudly' Podcast," *Chicago Tribune*, 2021, https://www.chicagotribune.com/lifestyles/ct-life-introvert-life-jeri-bingham-tt-0208-20210208-2r7dfjfc6vcj7hjrfprt6bwuhe-story.html.

outside of mainstream New Zealand culture. In his memoir, he writes about the hurdles of being an introvert and being an outsider by virtue of his accent and upbringing. These hurdles came on top of the challenges of being a senior politician, and staying authentic to himself as a quiet leader.[46] Further, there has been decades of social science research on how women (white or otherwise), even in positions of authority, are outsiders based on their perceptions and in reality. A female leader that's also a quiet leader certainly qualifies as a double outsider.[47]

My experience can highlight the challenges and opportunities of being a quiet leader and an outsider in other ways. I was born and raised to parents who immigrated from India in the 1970s. Relative to mainstream Americans, my family spoke a different language, practiced a different religion, ate different food, and thought about the world in a unique way colored by my parents' perspective of having grown up elsewhere. We also had to hold on to this culture with conviction. Living in a Chicago suburb in the 1980s, there wasn't nearly as much familiarity with or tolerance of something other than the mainstream as there is now (and even here we have work to do). Every part of being in American society, from learning how to celebrate the winter holidays, to dating in high school, to figuring out how to apply to college, required me to figure things out from scratch since nobody in the family had ever done these things before.

We will go into the challenges, but first it bears noting that being an outsider also has its advantages. Sticking to the values I've learned from my upbringing has been the bedrock of my work ethic and desire to make a positive impact on the world. Further, feeling like an outsider

---

[46] Simon Bridges, *National Identity: Confessions of an Outsider* (New York, NY: HarperCollins, 2021).

[47] Denise Cormier, "Why Top Professional Women Still Feel Like Outsiders," *Employment Relations Today* 33, no. 1 (2006): pp. 27–32, https://onlinelibrary. wiley.com/doi/abs/10.1002/ert.20095.

has been a major driver in my efforts as an entrepreneur. Having looked at the world differently my whole life, it's a natural extension for me to look at problems in health care in a different way as well. In addition, having to figure out how to live in mainstream society without much guidance is helpful when you're trying to operate in a new environment and do new, audacious things as an organization. It's a point of pride and motivation for me to advance my goals for my organizations without the benefit of prior connections, wealth, or a sense of how to operate in American society passed down to me from prior generations.

Indeed, there's value in focusing on the positive and thinking about the unique advantages of your differences. First, the benefits of being outside of the mainstream have helped quiet leaders including me subscribe to the belief that double outsiders can lead and lead effectively. Second, these characteristics can be a source of tangible advantage. These could be:

- The ability to generate unique insights with a perspective outside of the mainstream
- The resilience required to navigate society as an outsider
- The comfort with new situations that being an outsider can bring
- The ability to connect with other parts of our world and society that mainstream leaders can't

You may think of other ways that being a double outsider gives you advantages that nobody else can bring to the table. With the positives in mind, then next section goes into the potential hurdles of being a double outsider.

Specific Hurdles of Being a Quiet Leader and Double Outsider

Being a double outsider and quiet leader does have disadvantages that compound each other sometimes. My example and those of other quiet leaders illustrate how this can happen.

Connection

The distance (perceived or real) that double and triple outsiders feel between themselves and their colleagues makes it feel harder to build the one-on-one connections that flow into all aspects of leadership. Whether you are trying to build an understanding of the world, build your team, or share your vision and mission—how you find common ground with your collaborators is a critical element. This is already an area that requires focus and intention for quiet leaders. It can seem all the more daunting when you think you have less in common with your collaborators than others do.

This was especially true earlier in my career as I was working my way up the ranks. I already felt like an outsider in an extraverted culture as a quiet person trying to "fake it." On top of this, I was extremely aware of the feeling that I was not of the same world as my collaborators and mentors. This put even more distance between me and those I wanted to collaborate with and lead. This, in turn, made the goal of becoming a leader a more distant possibility. Perversely, it probably drove my desire to "fake it" even more, and that inauthenticity did not help me.

The companies I worked for cared about culture, and as such, sought to bring us together for outside activities. Ironically, this did as much to make me feel distance from my colleagues as anything that took place during working hours. I did not grow up surfing, skiing, playing golf, or partaking in any of the other activities that extraverts at organizations

I was a part of enjoyed doing at company events. Some of my extravert colleagues were carving up the ski slopes and holding court at the bar at company events. Meanwhile, I was focused on not trying to hurt myself on the bunny slopes after my first ski lesson, and then retreating to my room, exhausted by a full day of interacting with my peers.

When I did engage interpersonally with colleagues, in my own mind I felt I had fewer areas of common experience between me and my colleagues than they had between themselves. I also felt the distance from my colleagues when I compared my experience with that of extraverted colleagues that were outsiders in some way, culturally or otherwise. Relative to them, I felt disadvantaged as they had an innate ability to engage at the energy level of others that did not come naturally to me as a quiet leader. They were closer to the action because they could (in contrast to me), just "get out there" and try to find that common ground. Further, starting out as a young CEO of my first biotech, age become another barrier to connection. Along with being quiet, a minority, I was also over a decade younger than the median CEO in my industry. While the fifty-somethings in the room could trade stories about their kids in college and the music of the sixties and seventies, I both had to find unique ways to establish my credibility and also bridge the distance between myself and my collaborators. My unfamiliarity with pre-1980s pop culture is still a running joke on my teams to this day.

All this said, I am one of the lucky quiet leaders outside of the cultural mainstream. I grew up here in the extraverted culture of the United States, and at least I had a few areas of common ground to draw on with my counterparts from more mainstream backgrounds. Further, I had the benefit of an accent that sounded "American," which helps get your audience focused on the message. Other double outsiders come from cultures where the norm trends more toward quiet interaction with world, and both have to balance the strengths and weaknesses of their inherent nature and their upbringing as they broadcast their mission.

Lalitha, who we spoke about in Chapter 8, noted that being a triple outsider—the only woman, the only quiet leader, and the only minority in the group setting—compounded the challenges being heard, seen, and connecting with her team as a quiet leader. There was just so little she felt she had in common with others on her team, and it was hard enough already as an introvert for her to begin to engage them. These differences, on top of her quiet nature, felt discouraging as she sought to make an impact for her patients through leadership beyond the cultural, gender, and personality biases she felt she had to contend with in the workplace. Zhi, a C-level quiet leader in a software services company, originally grew up in China and learned to speak fluent English in preparation for and during graduate school in the United States. He has grown his ability to communicate over time through experience and training. Along his journey, he has noted the barriers that not speaking like a mainstream speaker can diminish the power of language (especially in the speaker's perception). Language barriers compound the effects of being a quiet leader, by adding additional hurdles to social interaction beyond their inward facing personalities. For example, especially earlier in his career, Zhi's self-consciousness about his accent often discouraged him from having the types of conversations that were critical to building connection with his colleagues. Sometimes, he would avoid attending company events altogether rather than avoid feeling further embarrassed by his perceived inability to connect.

Getting Noticed

Being different from the mainstream can sometimes get you noticed and make you memorable. Quiet leaders from non-majority backgrounds have observed that, ironically, being different sometimes makes it more difficult to get noticed in the ways that those from the mainstream do. Even though you stick out, even simple things like having a name that's more unfamiliar and difficult to pronounce can get in the way of having your reputation precede you in a good way. Also, preconceived notions related to your background can impact those that matter's ability to see you for your accomplishments.

I had this feeling of distance from the first time I would introduce myself to people. My name is inherently difficult to say for some and therefore harder for some people to remember. I remember, as valedictorian of my high school class, the teacher leading the graduation ceremony taking an excruciatingly long time to stumble through my last name during my introduction for a graduation speech. This happened even though I had met him probably a hundred times before that. Further, many times I'd be confused with someone else of Indian descent at the companies I have worked at, or sometimes be the only person in a group not referred to by name at all since my name was difficult to say. I have to admit that I am still mixed up with other South Asians at other companies I have founded, even by our own employees, despite my higher profile and long tenure. It's hard to stand out, get noticed, or be considered as a leader when folks can't remember who you are, especially for a quiet leader who has a harder time getting noticed from the outset.

Further, both Lalitha and Zhi noted that sometimes, preconceived notions about their race, gender, and culture preceded them in getting noticed. They felt they had a false version of themselves to counteract before folks really got a sense of their authentic selves, which was hard enough for them as introverts. For example, the stereotype of South Asian females as quiet and submissive, and East Asian individuals in general as quiet, detail-oriented, technically smart worker bees made each feel like they started at their organizations needing to work just to get back to zero base while making a name for themselves.

Broadcasting the mission

Some of the same barriers that challenge connection as a double outsider also affect how to connect with a broader audience when broadcasting your mission. The benefit of a unique background is the chance to tell a unique story that can grip your audience and focus them on your mission. The potential risk for a quiet leader from a non-mainstream background to contend with are unfortunately similar to those for one-on-one interactions. It sometimes feels—and can be—easier to connect with your audience when you look and sound like them. For quiet leaders, the idea that you are even further disadvantaged beyond your quiet nature can be daunting. Further, like for one-on-one connections, preconceived stereotypes can put a great onus on double outsiders to prove their credibility to the audience. This was true in Zhi's experience as he was learning to speak in groups—just the sense that you will go out there and be perceived as less credible and different is one more hurdle to overcome when focusing on the message during a presentation.

Where to go from here

For those of us who are from outside the mainstream stereotype of a leader, perhaps your heads were nodding reading my and other quiet leaders' stories above. Perhaps it made you angry at the way society and our leadership culture has been constructed. Zhi's, Lalitha's and my experiences perhaps made you more aware of the forces that you feel are conspiring against you in your ambition to lead. For those from the mainstream, you may have observed these phenomena, but are unsure what can be done about it given these are currents within the larger society we live in.

The double outsider leaders who have contributed to this book share one unifying theme. The distance created by difference may be part of our world, but we have some agency to navigate it and shape the organizations around us to account for it. When we take the opportunity to do something about this phenomenon (rather than approach the issue as victims), we jumpstart our ability to be effective leaders and do good in service of our missions.

One observation to place this phenomenon into context is that the distance being a double outsider may place between us and others is not unique to the actions of a particular employer or organization. It's rather a more ubiquitous part of living in a pluralistic society. I certainly felt the distance of being a double outsider at specific company events. However, I also felt this way, for example, at functions at my kids' school. Surprisingly to many, I felt even more like a fish out of water outside of work in low-stakes interactions. It's my version of a small private hell to be in a noisy room trying to make small talk with parents who didn't look like me and without my comfortable crutch of a common professional understanding to guide like it does at work. Indeed, distance between us and our mainstream colleagues and organizations is something we can seek to change. I liken the leadership climate for quiet leaders and those outside the mainstream to the weather: if it's raining where you go, the charge is to find the tools to not get wet. Let's dive into how quiet double outsiders have gone about seeking to shape the world around them to lead.

Using the Quiet Leader's Toolkit as a Quiet/Leader Double Outsider

The issues that cultural and other outsiders deal with on top of being quiet leaders are real barriers to leadership. So, what to do about it? This book's solution may be controversial: the same frameworks and tools that help quiet leaders from the mainstream are the right ones to help double outsiders be their most authentic selves as leaders. There is no special trick that can help a double outsider relative to other quiet leaders. If there were, you would be reading a very different book (or maybe two). What matters is which hurdles of quiet leadership to emphasize, and as such which tools to lean on the most. So, where are areas of particular focus for a "double outsider" when applying the Quiet Leader's Toolkit?

Emphasis on Transparency

Transparency in the Quiet Leader's toolkit plays a major factor in how double outsiders lead. There is a natural tendency for a quiet leader that feels the difference between themselves and their colleagues to retreat into themselves and hold their ideas and authentic selves even closer. That inner world is our comfort zone, and it can beckon when we think the world around us may judge us or penalize us for who we are. As a leader, however, not giving a window into yourself or staying in your inner world is not an option if you are to be effective.

As an outsider quiet leader, emphasizing that transparency of who you are, and how your organization runs has been, in my experience, the answer to closing the actual and my perceived distance between those I lead and me. As scary as that can be, giving people an authentic sense of who you are and what you stand for helps build trust, and ultimately that trust accrues to the work of connecting, learning, and broadcasting your message. The tools are there to use transparency to do the work of a leader in Chapters 4, 5, 6, and 7—the work of a double outsider is to practice these with intention and emphasis. Particularly when your unique background makes you inherently a bit harder to find common ground with than someone from the mainstream, being transparent maximizes the chance that others can relate to you. Further, that transparency and including people in your thought process and journey can set a tone that can multiply on itself. Giving people permission to be transparent creates reciprocity. Also, it starts a conversation that can build commonality. As unique as individuals are, I've often found I have more in common with colleagues from different backgrounds than I might have assumed.

Specifically, quiet leaders that are a part of this book have taken great intention to speak openly about their authentic selves. I speak openly about the different holidays I celebrate, foods I eat, and my nontraditional background. When I have an opportunity to go to a golf or ski event, I am transparent about why I might pass or participate with some modifications based on abject lack of experience on the slopes (my parents, coming from a warm country, were aghast at the idea of shelling out what little money we had to choose to be cold). My colleagues have taught me other ways to create transparency and embrace their differences—for example, an Orthodox Jewish investor of ours and introvert gave us some color into how he observes the Sabbath. It gave us a window into who he is and some understanding of how he needs to structure his work week. With this understanding, we can relate better to him as a person and also have more permission to share more of ourselves in return.

There is the ever-present danger that sharing these parts of yourself can lead to judgement or separation. If it does, that is data you can use to shape your organization, the people in it, or to find a new one. However, if you are not sharing your most authentic self, you have a lot lower chance of leading in the first place. Exercising judgement in how and when you share more than you typically otherwise would can help as you navigate this continuum. Start with more quotidian (holidays and food, for example) and relatable areas, and then you can work up to the heavier parts of your differences as you close your perceived distance with your colleagues.

Storytelling with transparency is another powerful way to build connection with a unique background either with individuals or with an entire audience. Your unique background gives you material that by definition will stand out in the crowd. The key is not to hide it but to embrace it and how it has affected you. Chapter 7 explored Tim Herbert's ability as a quiet leader to captivate the crowd through authentic story telling. One of his most powerful stories (it was for me when we spoke for this book) highlights Tim's "otherness," going deep on his intellectual disability and how he had to address it from a young age. What makes you as a quiet leader feel distant from others can actually be the most powerful way to connect with your audience. While it is scary, embracing it in your unique style and all of your perceived differences can be powerful.

Systems Thinking with Transparency in Mind

As leaders, building transparency into your overall organization can pay major dividends. As we talk about in Chapter 5, transparency drives efficiency, proactiveness, and your team's allegiance to the mission and trust in leadership. Double outsiders can take this transparency to an even higher level. For a double outsider leader that is at even higher risk of being seen as mysterious, aloof, and difficult to know, being open with what you know (obviously with the right caveats), where the organization is headed, and what you think about people helps in a few ways. It helps a quiet leader combat any internal sense of the distance between them and colleagues; by creating a culture of sharing, you can take some agency in closing the gap. Further, it is the antidote to the potential misperceptions that come with being out of the mainstream. It is harder to be misunderstood if you are putting your cards on the table. Chapter 5 gives some specific suggestions on how you can build transparency into the processes of your business, through planned communication, empowerment of those on your team, and how you communicate with your team. For a double outsider, the signal that an organization values transparency also gives the entire organization more agency to be more transparent (as this is what the boss values). This, in turn, can close the distance between the quiet leaders and extraverts, and the outsiders and those from a more traditional cultural background.

Collaboration with Transparency

You can enlist colleagues and mentors in supporting your efforts to bridge diversity to create connection. Leaders, boards, and mentors must run their organizations to make space for the double and triple outsiders in their ranks. If we don't, we risk tapping the same types of leaders to lead over and over again. In an increasingly diverse and complex world, a lack of diversity in the leadership ranks can be a risk even beyond the exclusion of quiet leaders.

Specifically, even if you are not a double outsider, setting a tone organizationally that encourages transparency about our differences can help make space for how quiet leadership and other elements of diversity intersect. This has to go beyond the formulaic diversity trainings and cookie cutter twitter posts about how diverse companies can be. It needs to be wired deeply into the organization. For example, emphasizing hiring and training employees that are authentically curious and open to new people and ideas can make space for double outsiders. It can also mean celebrating a company's culture in ways that are more accessible to all, quiet or not, mainstream or not. For example, rather than a one-size-fits-all activity like a bar night, an outing with multiple choices that allow one to select the level of interaction intensity can help. Choice of activity can make a difference too; a cooking class may be a better bet than a golf outing (after all, regardless of who you are and where you come from, you have to eat). As another example, a day of community service focuses the group on a task that are common to all (raking leaves to clean up a park, sorting holiday gifts for the needy); it's also another way to allow the quiet leaders and extraverts to select tasks best suited for them.

Also, cultivation of empathy for what double outsiders go through can go a long way. This includes setting a good personal example for the team to follow. Even if you are not a double outsider, the transparency and openness about your differences you set as a leader creates permission for others to follow your lead. For example, as we explore in Chapters 5 and 8, making space for not just quiet leaders, but also those of different cultures to share their ideas can make a difference. For example, for someone who may be newer to the English language, allowing them time to prepare or share their thoughts in writing first can increase comfort level with sharing their opinions in the group setting. Extraverts and those from more mainstream cultural backgrounds can help quiet leaders immensely simply by taking a minute to acknowledge their double outsider peers, and their unique perspective and challenges. Because few people have the same experience as they do, double outsiders often contend with the opportunities and challenges of their background individually. Being seen by the group can be a huge unifier.

The experience of quiet leaders that are double outsiders highlights the power of the Quiet Leader's Toolkit in helping quiet leaders of all backgrounds access leadership more authentically. Now, the book will dive into, for all quiet leaders, where to go from here and putting the Toolkit into practice.

Chapter 10

Concluding Thoughts— Putting it Into Practice

You may have ascended to leadership already and are looking to expand your effectiveness as your organization grows. You may also be aspiring to leadership now that you've identified yourself as a quiet leader. You have reviewed the key tasks on the leader's checklist, the Quiet Leader's Toolkit, and the frameworks for how quiet leaders can best address them. Now where do we go from here? We'll dive into how we can use the Toolkit to put these ideas into practice.

The Power of Systematic Thinking: Setting Up Your System to Grow as a Leader

Like improving anything, building on your leadership practices takes a system. Both common sense, and social science suggest that relying on your individual will power to change your behavior from what you are doing to what you should do is unlikely to be successful. Making behavioral changes by designing and following a multi-part system can be far more effective and comprehensive. The simple example of this is the idea of a commitment device (such as paying for a yearlong gym membership to incentivize you to exercise) that can help reinforce non-preferred but beneficial behaviors; multiple studies have shown their effectiveness changing even highly ingrained behaviors, like smoking.[48] How can you build a system around you to drive your growth as a quiet leader?

Defining your intentions: Before beginning the journey to grow as a quiet leader, it's important to reflect on why you're doing this. The *why* of ascending to leadership, or growing one's leadership is critical, as it will be your source of inspiration when things don't go as planned. Quiet leaders by nature are less driven by external incentives than are extraverts. Finding that inner reason you want to deliver more to your organization is a key first step to ensuring that your journey is sustainable. The *why* will also keep you grounded as the demands both internal to your organization and outside begin to multiply.

Focusing your efforts: Choose one or two key tasks you'd like to improve at a time. Taking on improvement on many fronts at once can be overwhelming and likely ineffective given the weight of the day-to-day tasks of leading. It's worth revisiting the self-reflection questions we considered in Chapter 3 to start taking inventory of where to focus. For example, like Senator Brownsberger, you may be extremely strong at connecting one-on-one but you may want to focus on how you build a following in a group setting. Or, like Lathika, you might be great at building an understanding of the world around you but

---

[48]   Katherine Milkman, Todd Rogers, and Max H. Bazerman. "Harnessing Our Inner Angels and Demons: What We Have Learned about Want/Should Conflicts and How That Knowledge can Help us Reduce Short-Sighted Decision Making." *Perspectives on Psychological Science* 3, no. 4 (2008): 324–38. https://doi.org/10.1111/j.1745-6924.2008.00083.x.

want to work more on how you show up to collaborate with extraverts in a peer setting.

To put this into practice, we can revisit and amplify the questions to ask from Chapter 3.

- Which tasks of leadership do you practice those most in your day to day?
- Which ones are strengths?
- Which ones are most challenging for you as a quiet leader and why? You can define challenge by whether you objectively think you're succeeding t them, and which ones feel most "natural."
- What specific actions can I take over time to find my authentic way of practicing these tasks?

It's also important to revisit these priorities over time, as what's required of you as a current or potential leader evolves, and as you make progress on your priorities. For example, as some of the businesses I have led have grown, I've had to turn my attention toward building my capabilities to build a following at scale, whereas previously I was more focused on one-on-one connections that were most appropriate for a smaller team and enterprise.

Committing your preferred behaviors to routine

For many of these key tasks, there is a way to set to time the key activities required to grow. For example, you can commit to the calendar a number of times per year that you go to meetings, cocktail parties, and other unstructured group events. You can also commit to the calendar the preparation steps that we've discussed in prior chapters to make the most out of these individual interactions or public speaking engagements. For those quiet leaders trying to deepen their understanding of the world, you can make a target list of experts to build and maintain connections with and work down that list over a reasonable period of time.

Measuring results

How will you know that you are seeing results as you focus on those areas? The answer flows from some of the lessons of Chapter 5. Coupling this strategy with a method to measure your efforts is a key part of a systems approach to leadership growth. There are both input and output driven measures. Input measures are often attractive as they are 100 percent within your control—for example, number of speaking engagements you take in a given year, or the number of follow-up discussions you have after a networking event. Output measures are attractive as they dovetail your focus areas for improvement with what you're ultimately graded on as a leader: results. An example of a results-oriented measure could be the number of one-on-one connections you have that result in a positive follow-up (another meeting, an introduction, or a sale).

Qualitative measures can also be useful—for example, how you feel (comfortable, within your authentic self or not for example) and your intuition into how your counterpart feels as you exhibit vulnerability is qualitative. The Toolkit component of collaboration is quite useful to get the best data. Teammates and trusted colleagues can help as their insights can sometimes be more objective than your own because you may be viewing your results through a more self-critical lens. Enlisting them as part of 360 feedback or as mentors and colleagues can be a helpful way to learn and course-correct as needed.

Finding collaborators and exercising vulnerability

Indeed, mentors and collaborators are a crucial part of taking action to grow your skills. They can give you honest feedback, and might be quiet leaders themselves. Other quiet leaders can relate to the unique opportunities and challenges you face, and they can also legitimize the quiet personality type in a world that glorifies extraversion. I have used the quiet leaders on the teams I have worked with as sounding boards as I've looked to grow my leadership style. Quiet leaders by nature tend to be observant and understand from their own experience what you're trying to accomplish. Collaboration is most effective when coupled with transparency from the Toolkit. When I took the step to be open about my challenges as a quiet leader, it opened up many new opportunities for me to learn. With some guidance on what I am working on as a leader, my teammates have supported me with targeted feedback. They have told me directly when I might be too deep within my thoughts and appear aloof during a meeting, and have pulled me aside when less could be more as I try to match the energy of an extravert. You may even share some of the strategies you are using to measure your efforts in case that helps your collaborators frame how they're seeing you progress. If you are senior leader of an organization, it will take some effort to solicit this feedback. The more senior you are, the less people underneath you feel they have to gain by pointing out your flaws. Your commitment to humility and transparency for your organization can help set the tone.

Approaching your goals with self-compassion

Just as important as the system is exercising self-compassion. It is important to be mindful that growth can take time, energy, and patience. Stepping out of our comfort zones as quiet leaders is hard—as is the trial and error of experimenting with styles that work for you until you get it right. I and the other quiet leaders sharing our stories have had our share of face-palm moments, where looking back, a style that I tried did not create the intended results. Ironically, the humanity to be wrong and fail can be an important part of creating a culture as a leader. If we embrace it authentically, learn from it, and show those we lead around us that we've grown, others will do so as well in your organizations. This has helped contribute to the culture of self-improvement that I continue to promote in every organization I have helped build.

Looking Forward

Leading, at its most elevated form, is about investing in yourself to create something larger than yourself. It is at times inspiring when you accomplish great things. Leadership can also be demoralizing when you fall short of your expectations because it always require full engagement and all of yourself. Ultimately, given the enormity of the exercise, leadership is only sustainable, as the quiet leaders supporting this book found, when you practice it in a way authentic to you. Many of us can play a role that our extraverted society asks us to, but it robs us of sustainability, and most importantly, the joy of working with others to accomplish something great.

Even if you can fake it and go toe to toe with the extraverts, this is seldom any fun. When things aren't fun, we tend to not do them. This is a major loss for society. If only certain people, with certain backgrounds, beliefs, and personalities lead, we would all be worse off. As complex as this world is, we need diverse leadership to tackle the diverse challenges we face as a society in creative ways. Excluding people that have a unique way of interacting with the world does quiet leaders a disservice and robs us of creative new ideas that can make things better. What I wish for all of us is that we find great things to build, grow, and lead. Further, I wish for all of us that when we lead, we do it with joy and self-compassion.

Further, I wish that we all take on the highs and lows of leadership with the certainty that there's no one way to be a great leader, and that we've found the right way for us.

On behalf of my collaborators on this endeavor, I hope that the practical suggestions in this book can help you on that journey to refine your style and practice it in a way that feels true to yourself. I wish you great success in finding your stride as a quiet leader, and I am excited about the great things you will do for yourself, the people around you, and our society at large.

About the Author

Ankit Mahadevia is the Founder and CEO of Spero Therapeutics, an organization committed to fighting the threat of infectious disease through the development of novel medicines. Over his career, he has led the formation of nine companies, including Spero, several of which are trading on the Nasdaq exchange and several others acquired by large pharmaceutical organizations. Through these companies, he has raised over $1 billion for development of novel therapeutics, and built multiple high performing management teams. He and the companies he has built have won multiple awards for their culture, including *Boston Business Journal's* "Best Places to Work" Award and Glassdoor's "Top 50 CEOs of 2021" (#15 nationwide).

Prior to these roles, Ankit has advised on and supported investments into the biotechnology sector as a Venture Partner at Atlas Venture, a Cambridge, MA, venture capital firm. He has held previous positions at organizations including Genentech, McKinsey & Company, the United States Government Accountability Office, and the U.S. Senate Health, Education, Labor, and Pensions Committee.

He has spoken widely on entrepreneurship and leadership, including at Harvard University, Columbia University, Northwestern University, MIT, and the Berkeley Forum. Ankit received his medical degree from the Johns Hopkins University School of Medicine, an MBA from the Wharton School at the University of Pennsylvania, and a BA from Northwestern University. He lives in Chestnut Hill, MA, with his wife and two sons.

CPSIA information can be obtained
at www.ICGtesting.com
Printed in the USA
BVHW091621180922
647078BV00005B/14

9 781637 582893